Simple Sustainable Living

Environmentally Friendly Hacks for Saving Money,
Becoming Self-Sufficient, and Living a Zero-Waste Lifestyle

Taylor Sampson

This book is dedicated to my parents, who taught me to appreciate what I have and never be wasteful

Table of Contents

Introduction.. ix

1 What is Sustainable Living? 1

Sustainability Pillars 5

Is Sustainable Living Important?........................ 11

Sustainably Saves You Money and Is Not Expensive 14

It's So Easy; You Can Start Today 15

A Sustainable Mindset 16

Environmentalism vs. Conservationism 17

2 A Sustainable Lifestyle................................. 19

Sustainable Transportation 20

Thrift Shopping.. 24

Can You Achieve a Low-Impact Home?....... 27

Burial Pods: Eco-Conscious Funerals 28

How To Transition to Low-Impact Living.........29

3 The 5 Rs 31

Zero-Waste Lifestyle... 32

The 5 Rs 33

4 Sustainability Through DIY..................................... 43

DIY and Save!..44

Kickstart Your DIY Journey With These Easy Projects...48

DIY Beauty..50

DIY Cleaning Products..53

5 Going and Growing Green in Cities.......................... 57

Backyard Income 58

Getting Started 60

Year-Round Growth 65

Planting Location 65

Grow Veggies Indoors 67

A Pest Problem 68

Create a Safe-Haven for Pollinators..........................72

Become an Urban Beekeeper..72

Store Your Harvest..74

6 A Healthy Diet—the Organic Way............................. 79

The Future Is Organic..80

Why Organic Food? 81

Get Invested in an Eco-Friendly Diet..........................82

A Sustainable Eating Plan 85

The Danger of Microplastics 88

How to Enjoy a Nutritious Vegetarian Diet....................89

7 Be Water Wise 93

Why Your Water Meter Is Running Fast..........................94

Water Conservation 96

Water Harvesting.. 98

8 Conserve Energy.. 103

An Energy-Efficient Home 104

Renewable Energy Is the Best Way to Power
Your Home.. 107

The Future Is Powered by Solar Power 113

Get Ahead of the Cold... 115

Conclusion.. 117

Leave a Review... 119

References...121

Introduction

Refuse what you do not need; reduce what you do need; reuse what you consume; recycle what you cannot refuse, reduce, or reuse; and rot (compost) the rest.

- Bea Johnson

People's concern for the environment is on the rise. A sustainable life is at the forefront of your mind as climate change takes center stage as one of today's more pressing issues. "In the US, in November 2019, two in three Americans (66%) said they were at least 'somewhat worried' about global warming, an increase of 10 percentage points over the past five years" (Painter & Andı, 2020). With concern on the increase, I know you want to learn ways that you can become more sustainable in your home and everyday life.

You are not alone: 77% of individuals today want to know what they can do to live a more sustainable life (Ellsmoor, 2019). Hence, information needs to be readily available to meet this desire. Unfortunately, getting lost in a sea of information about sustainability and a more self-reliant lifestyle is easy.

If you purchased this book, you have been searching for a simple, cohesive guide that will lead you to increased self-reliance. You want to reach a point where your household produces minimal to zero waste by growing your food and reducing what you throw away. Plastic is a pain point for any environmentally-friendly home; therefore, I know you want to limit your dependence on it. You want to know how to recycle and reuse items you buy and information about preserving food, renewable energy, and minimizing your CO_2 footprint. This is the information I want to impart to you through this book.

Extreme weather variations have become the norm. The climate is also changing at an unbelievable rate that may even scare you as you wonder how that will impact your life or those of the next generation. You might already be searching for ways to reduce your carbon emission and how to save money doing that effectively. You envision your own space to grow vegetables, keep chickens, or have bees to make honey. It may be one of your desires to grow your own food, but you find you cannot due to the unavailability of farming land and off-grid properties. You probably are actively searching for simple steps to take in your home to save money and still achieve sustainability so that you can live a healthy life.

One person cannot defeat pollution and climate change, but if you make small changes in your life, you can help the environment in your own small way. You should not feel guilty if you cannot do everything possible to heal the planet or make your household the gold standard of zero-waste living, but this book will provide you with basic solutions to start combating it. The more steps you take, the more you will want to take and the easier it becomes. Indeed, you will look forward to the satisfaction and the flavors you enjoy from growing your own food, even if it is only a few herbs on the window sill, and you will begin to take notice of packaging and purchasing options that are more environmentally friendly.

I understand these environmental issues you're struggling with because I have pondered over the same problems. Not only that, but because I have studied wildlife biology, I understand the negative impacts climate change has had on the earth's ecosystems. I was exactly like you; I did not have extensive farming land to live off-grid, but I was determined to change my lifestyle despite being in an urban area.

You may look up to those who have committed to a zero-waste lifestyle and are self-reliant; being like them was my goal when I formulated many of the habits I will reveal to you in this book. I asked myself how they managed to get by without the seemingly necessary daily conveniences I had relied on all my life. I realized that to make a significant change; you have to make a series of more minor changes. Numerous little steps can carry you to a new destination, and until I understood that, I felt stuck. If you are in the same place, I get it. Trust me—you can start making strides in your sustainability journey today without becoming overwhelmed.

When you finish reading *Simple Sustainable Living*, you will have a new perspective on what it means to be self-reliant. Not only will you learn about preserving food, but you will also learn skills related to gardening without acres of land, making financially sound decisions using the 5 Rs of zero waste, and incorporating a healthy diet to reinforce healthy and more sustainable habits.

I have spent nearly a decade experimenting with the eco-friendly methods interspersed throughout the pages of this book. What I learned did not come to me overnight. I experienced a lot of trial and error before finding ways that were effective for my situation. My passion for conserving the environment began long before I completed my doctorate in wildlife biology. I decided to do my best to help others lower trash and cash output. Because of the knowledge I have collected, I am confident that following the guidance in this book will improve your chances of successfully switching to a more sustainable lifestyle.

Imagine getting your own produce from your garden to prepare delicious meals for yourself or your family without using a vehicle and money to visit a grocery store to purchase fresh produce there. Imagine an existence where you don't have to worry about the toxic load from beauty or cleaning products because you have made your own safe products at home. What if you could curb your water use and save energy by making your home more energy efficient? What if you could live sustainably until the day you die and be buried as part of a tree? Does this appeal to you? These are just a few of the opportunities you will learn about from reading this book.

Simple Sustainable Living is a product of numerous sources of information. I had to scour relevant publications and keep my eye on environmental developments, policies, and laws to keep my information accurate. It would be best if you didn't run into the same obstacles that I did, and I don't want your sustainability journey to become frustrating or too complicated; that is why I have written this book. At the same time, I want you to enjoy this book and not feel that you are an evil person destroying our environment if you don't do every hack in this book. A lot of these hacks I don't do myself, either because I can't or because I have friends that already do, and they give me sustainable gifts, or I trade with them. I am committed to the environment, but this book contains suggestions and ideas, not demands. I hope you will find this journey toward a more sustainable lifestyle fun as I have.

You will have a seamless crossover into an eco-friendlier lifestyle through the following chapters. If you were previously trying to figure out how to start being more environmentally conscious, this book is a wonderful beginning. Remember to keep an open mind and think outside the box as you go through the innovative ideas provided for you. Because you may need more traditional tools to go off-grid, you need to remain creative and push the envelope with the solutions you implement. Some suggestions may feel out of the ordinary, but go with the flow, and you will make significant changes leading to a zero-waste lifestyle that is enviable to even the most experienced, self-reliant person.

1

What is Sustainable Living?

The word "sustainability" has become a buzzword when speaking about environmental matters, but do you know what it means exactly? I took its meaning for granted and thought it was self-explanatory until I became invested in this lifestyle. Living this way has so many layers, including more than just recycling.

The old school version of sustainability was reduce, reuse, recycle, but the concept has evolved further as climate change has worsened. Sustainability is more than just a noun; unpacking what this lifestyle is about opened my eyes to its true meaning. "According to sustainable facts, about 80% of the items Americans throw away can be recycled. However, currently, America's recycling rate is only 28%" (Stella, n.d.).

This low recycling rate means we need more people to try to live an environmentally conscious lifestyle. However, a lack of action is only sometimes intentional. Sometimes, people may need the correct information to make more informed decisions. Maybe that was the situation for you, too. Luckily, you are on a better path now because reading this book will empower you to make changes and better choices.

Chapter 1 will teach you what the real meaning of sustainable living is. Beyond learning the definition of a sustainable life, you will also learn the pillars of sustainability and why the lifestyle is indispensable. There is a misconception that a sustainable life is difficult to implement. Still, this part of the book will debunk that and illustrate how easy it is to make meaningful changes.

When done right, going green can save you a significant amount of money (Jabs, 2012), which will be discussed as the chapter unfolds. Changing how you do things requires persistence, determination, and commitment. You have to be in the right mindset to continue making sound decisions, but when you do, you not only help the well-being of the environment and become more independent but also save money.

This first chapter will also delve into the mindset you should adopt to lead a zero-waste life. I used to think that conservation and environmentalism are the same things, but there are subtle differences that can enhance the meaning of what a sustainable life is. Discussing these distinctions will conclude the chapter, giving you a holistic view of what sustainable living is. So, let's get into it.

Sustainable living has a rich history in modern culture. It has gained popularity worldwide and for a good reason. Many celebrities like Rhianna and Leonardo DiCaprio have invested in the sustainability movement (Hirsh, 2022). However, ordinary people can adopt eco-conscious habits in our day-to-day lives too. Large corporations can also take on sustainability by integrating sustainable living into their business practices and client relations.

In simple terms, sustainable living means not creating unnecessary waste and squandering natural resources to the detriment of future generations. The emphasis is primarily on utilizing natural and renewable resources. Another perspective on sustainable living is to meet your basic needs for water, food, and shelter without plundering the environment and leaving nothing for future generations.

Things in short supply (for example, fossil fuels) should be used wisely. The focus should be on resources that can be replaced or replenished, like solar and wind energy. The world over, people have come up with ingenious ways of implementing sustainable living to save money and reduce their energy footprint.

Firstly, you can make your home more eco-friendly, regardless of the type of home you live in. Keeping your home warm or cool throughout the year to cope with the changing seasons can cause problems with air quality and consume far more energy than necessary. To combat this, consider improving the insulation in your home so that there is less need for air conditioning or heating, which will also reduce the amount of energy you use daily. Additionally, installing energy-efficient windows can significantly affect your energy consumption. Finally, if you cannot afford extensive renovations, making your own draft blockers and storm windows can not only help the environment but your pocketbook too.

Secondly, consider reusing and recycling to reduce your rate of consumption. Donate items you no longer need and are in good condition to those less fortunate or loved ones who may need them. If the item is broken or can no longer be used, consider learning how to recycle it appropriately. You can compost your vegetable or fruit scraps (organic waste) or take your food waste to communal collection points that are increasingly becoming more common.

Recycle food packaging that is either glass, paper, or plastic. The world is becoming reliant on electronic gadgets, so electronic waste is also rising. Find out where to get rid of electronic waste locally to be reused or recycled instead of dumping it. Even your clothes can be recycled into other items or given to charities that can pass them on to those in need.

Lastly, try only to consume food from producers who practice sustainable production. Ideally, you would want to choose a producer who considers sustainability, from how they source the food to how they process, package, and deliver it for your consumption. You can check the label to see if it has a sustainable certification label on it to ensure you are not supporting food producers who harm the environment, but if possible, take the time to research products labeled sustainable. Because sustainable production can cost more labor, some unethical companies will take advantage of the label to charge you more even though they don't meet the criteria of a sustainable product (Will from Holland, n.d.).

The above three examples illustrate sustainable living, although it is not an exhaustive list. Now that you have an idea of what sustainable living can be, perhaps you are wondering about its importance—the why serves as the last motivation to encourage you to make the change.

Obviously, some resources are finite, so we must be careful how we use them. I want to promote sustainability to help limit the over-exploitation of critical natural resources. Not considering the consequences of waste can mean that we consume the earth's resources at a rate that will make the environment hostile to humans. There is no planet "B," and despite our fantastic imaginations, it is improbable that we will find one. It is even more unlikely that we will be capable of making one before we become extinct ourselves.

Sustainable living describes a lifestyle designed to help current generations leave the earth in the same or better condition for those who come after. Our environment needs to be able to sustain how we live. We need to use water in a way that doesn't overwhelm fresh water supplies and consume food in ways that do not cause land degradation or threaten ecological diversity.

With the way things are now, will future generations get a chance to enjoy the resources people at this time take for granted? "According to the UN Environment Program, if the global population reaches 9.6 billion by 2050, we could need "the equivalent of almost three planets...to provide the natural resources needed to sustain current lifestyles"" (Cheesman, 2020, para. 9).

The urgency needed to move people towards sustainable lifestyle habits cannot be overstated. The longer people take to understand what a zero-waste life is about, the less time we have to stop the damage and find solutions before that damage becomes irreversible. The changes can seem inconvenient initially, but they can become your norm. Going the extra mile to do the right thing for yourself and everyone else will make you feel good about your eco-friendly decisions. Recognize that small changes can go a long way and inspire others to join the effort.

Sustainability Pillars

Issues surrounding sustainability cannot be solved in a vacuum. A country facing significant economic and political problems cannot focus on and achieve its environmental goals. Unfortunately, if they do not focus on sustainability, the urgency surrounding ecological issues, often not seen as a priority, can become a negative feedback loop.

When we think about sustainability, we can imagine it as a roof with three pillars to hold it up. The sustainability roof protects its occupants from environmental issues threatening their quality of life. The three pillars represent social, economic, and environmental conditions (Brundtland, 1987). Another name for these pillars is "The 3 Ps of Sustainability" (people, profit, planet) or "The Triple Bottom Line."

It is only through a combination of these three pillars that sustainability is achieved. These three pillars interact with one another. Recognizing their interdependence gives a deeper understanding of how they affect your life. Initially, the three pillars were envisioned as equal but interdependent. More sophisticated interpretations now recognize a hierarchy, where the economy is contained in society and society is contained within the environment (Rinalducci, 2022). Combining economic and environmental sustainability makes your living conditions viable and is only threatened by social unrest. If you mix social and economic sustainability, your living conditions become bearable if you have enough money to maintain the lifestyle. If you combine social and environmental sustainability, your living conditions will become equitable with everyone else's until the environment can no longer sustain life on Earth. This is why the pillars are interdependent.

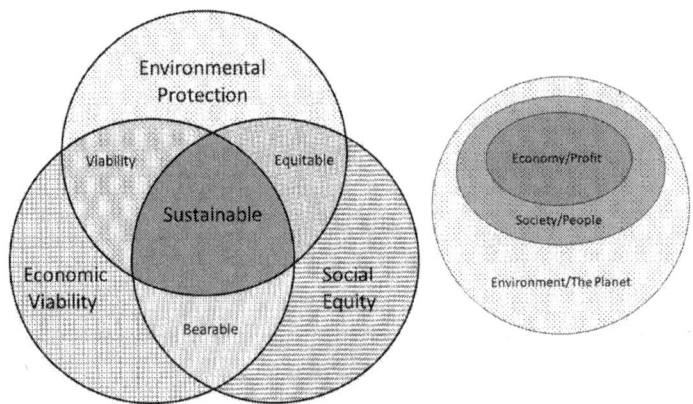

The three pillars of sustainability; the traditional concept where the pillars are equal, and the more modern concept, with a hierarchy. Both consider the pillars interdependent.

Social Equity (People)

The social pillar of sustainability includes a variety of factors, including social justice, maintaining peace, fighting poverty, and promoting diversity. Keeping your quality of life, access to healthcare and education, and protecting your cultural heritage also fall under the social equity pillar.

This pillar mainly concerns the regulations and public policies that maintain and support the social issues mentioned above. Compared to the other two pillars, it is not very defined or vaguely understood. However, the social pillar is essential because it can influence how we behave, individually and as a society.

Security, human rights, and world peace are all essential aspects of social sustainability. War and crime inevitably hurt the natural environment. Weapons of war distribute a number of pollutants; war tactics normalize unethical practices and desensitize humans to what is acceptable. People that are victims of war, human rights violations, crime, and other corrupt practices will find it challenging to maintain a sustainable lifestyle.

Access to healthcare is also a primary aspect of social sustainability. For example, suppose you have limited access to healthcare. In that case, you may need to drive more to treat conditions that could have been prevented if treated sooner.

Personal wealth is distributed unevenly across the world. Indeed, the wealthiest 2% of adults own more than 50% of the world's assets, while the poorest half hold only 1% of the wealth. Furthermore, it is estimated that the USA, which comprises about 4.5% of the world's population, consumes 25% of its energy. Similarly, figures for material, water, and food consumption display significant levels of disparity between the richest and poorest countries (FutureLearn, 2020). This disparity in social equity is an obstacle to sustainability worldwide.

Societies with high poverty or low social justice rates do not have the resources and foresight to make long-term sustainability plans, which ultimately harms the community and its environment. Cultural and religious influences can cause society to become more socially and environmentally conscious. Suppose a religious or cultural leader calls on a community to adopt certain practices. In that situation, they can influence followers to change their habits, which can benefit sustainable development. A notable example is Pope Francis and the Dalai Lama calling for the preservation of ecosystems and joining hands to fight ecological degradation. The above aspects exemplify social sustainability and how it can affect your quality of life and your community.

Economic Sustainability (Profit)

This pillar of sustainability deals with the essential aspects that need to be present for a business to exist. To be economically viable, a business must be able to sustain itself while making a profit. Profit is essential to economic sustainability, but business leaders should look at it more holistically.

Social and environmental factors should be considered along with profit and other economic factors. Although it is wise to factor in different aspects, such as the environment, businesses often need to pay more attention to the availability of natural resources. This oversight compromises long-term economic growth. The capitalist mindset works by assuming there's always an opportunity to make more profit. With this way of thinking, there is no consideration for the limitations surrounding finite resources until they are nearly depleted. Investors often drive the system. For example, they can invest in old-growth timber, maximize profit, and when it's all gone, take their money and invest it somewhere else. It is not the stockholders who lose their jobs and have to live next to the clear-cut.

Businesses that use unsustainable methods to turn a profit are often minimally fined or given a light slap on the wrist while their earnings are maintained. Unfortunately, it is unusual for there to be an economic benefit given to businesses that adopt eco-friendly practices. The best way to persuade companies not to use environmentally harmful practices is to introduce taxes and levies for waste, provide incentives for sustainable business methods that favor the preservation of the environment, and for consumers to use the power of their purchasing choices.

Therefore, business is not driven by righteous virtues but rather by the bottom line. This is not going to change, but you can affect the bottom line. Luckily, in recent times, the world has begun to realize that sustainable business practices are important in the private and public sectors. More and more people are refusing to do business with corporations that do not have a sustainable business model. A reputation for being environmentally harmful can negatively impact a business's brand and pressure them to adopt a more eco-friendly strategy. This doesn't mean that profit no longer drives enterprise, but enterprise can be influenced by social consciousness because it ultimately affects the bottom line. They are becoming more environmentally responsible and working toward improving their economic and environmental sustainability because the culture is changing.

Environmental Sustainability (Planet)

The environmental pillar regulates and manages natural resources like land, wildlife, forests, and freshwater. This encompasses any kind of regulation or legal restriction that aims to protect the environment. The efforts under the environmental pillar are to preserve the environment and involve those that control human consumption.

To manage the environment adequately, there is a need for expert knowledge in conservation biology and environmental science. When you look at the kind of activities a country must manage, like allocating water and land, a high level of expertise is necessary. At a national level, the emissions of the entire nation need to be considered to ascertain if the environmental management strategies are working. Managing the environment also considers how durable ecosystems are to disruptions resulting from humans' actions.

Another way to maintain this pillar is to keep tight control over the resources that humans use to carry out their daily activities. Energy consumption should be kept to a minimum, and there should be incentives for using renewable resources and saving energy. Properly planned cities put more thought into making them sustainable for their occupants.

Products or goods should be used so that their lifespan is circular to enjoy their full benefits (reused or recycled) instead of ending up in landfills after being used once. Being sustainable also includes ensuring that population growth does not exceed a rate where the resources available cannot adequately meet the people's basic needs in a particular area. Currently, the trend is that the populations of developed countries are in a slight decline or stable, while in developing countries, populations are increasing. Those in developing countries should also have a good standard of living and equality, which can contribute to minimizing the growth rate of the population.

The kind of food you eat and the diet you maintain go a long way in ensuring that the environment is protected. A sustainable diet is one where meat or animal products are not the main focus. Further, CO2 emissions should be reduced by only focusing on using renewable resources, staying efficient, and keeping abreast of new technologies and development.

The way you use freshwater can either compromise or contribute to a sustainable lifestyle. You must manage how you use fresh water and keep things innovative and up-to-date according to new green technologies. Agriculture uses a lot of water, so you should be cognizant of how you utilize this precious resource during agricultural activities.

These are just a few examples of what environmental sustainability entails. Hopefully, the three pillars are useful in helping you to understand better sustainability and how to have a more eco-friendly lifestyle.

Is Sustainable Living Important?

Sustainable living means that you exist on the planet with a sense of responsibility to use its resources wisely so that future generations can enjoy a good quality of life with the available resources. As it stands, we rely on fossil fuels as an energy source; this reliance keeps our carbon footprint high and harms the environment. Sustainable living requires individuals (and, therefore, businesses) to discharge their moral obligation not to put profits and selfish economic desires above preserving the environment. Although this type of lifestyle positively impacts the environment, it can also make improvements that benefit you directly. The following benefits can come about when you lead a sustainable lifestyle.

Saves You Money

Some people are motivated by how change affects their bank balance. The good news is that environmental sustainability not only benefits the earth, but it can also save you some money. For example, an efficient and sustainable household means lower utility bills.

Indeed, you may be able to permanently eradicate any utility bill by using renewable energy sources like solar power. Buying locally-produced organic food with no disposable packaging may be cheaper; less food waste means you save money because you only buy what you need. Using an electric car or public transport can reduce your fuel bill. Sustainable living can also reduce your medical bills due to the health benefits you will accrue from the lifestyle.

Keeps You Healthy

If you are motivated by how sustainable living will affect your well-being, you will be pleased to know that your health may change positively. Sustainable living may improve the air quality of your surroundings, resulting in you inhaling fewer toxins. A sustainable life means eating the right food and reducing the consumption of red meat and processed foods, improving your health, and reducing your chances of developing chronic diseases. Keeping your body weight within the normal range and partaking in cardiovascular exercise (aerobic activity like brisk walking, running, or cycling) also contributes to keeping your body in the best shape possible. Unfortunately, plastic waste finds its way into the food we eat and the water we drink. By using reusable bottles, packaging, and bags, you may be able to reduce the amount of plastic waste that ends up in your food.

Preserves the Environment and Safeguards Natural Resources

In the last 50 years, the lifestyle most people have been leading, coupled with industrialization, has negatively impacted the environment. If we want to slow the effects of this damage and climate change, we must start living sustainably immediately.

With sustainable living, what we dump in our oceans and other bodies of water will be reduced. There will also be more pressure to monitor waste so that fewer toxins are released into them. When we all embrace sustainable living, greenhouse gases will be kept to a minimum, slowing climate change. You can do your part to minimize plastic pollution by refusing to use plastic products. The way you use natural resources should keep them available for future generations. A sustainable life will ensure that natural resources are conserved so that future generations can live as comfortably as we do today.

Secures a Sustainable Economy

Sometimes it is hard, during the day-to-day struggle, to keep the future of coming generations at the forefront of the mind. Sustainability as a concept is relatively new. Therefore, the technology is also new. So much potential economic development is yet to occur, which means green jobs are being created as more investment is poured into sustainability.

Local communities benefit from the preservation of the environment and the jobs being created to save natural resources. Recycling can put the power back into the hands of local businesses that repurpose materials so that new ones don't need to be acquired. An empowered community that uses fewer nonrenewable resources makes for better economic sustainability.

Reduces Energy Usage

Some suggestions for sustainable living include switching to energy-efficient lighting, using solar or wind energy in your home and business, or using energy-efficient machinery and equipment. These green initiatives may reduce energy usage in the long run, and the month-to-month energy bill reduction may lead to significant savings, which will help with sustainability overall.

The benefits of sustainable living can help get the conversation started to reduce energy usage in your community if the conversation is not already happening. Different things drive people. Some will be spurred into action when you tell them the statistics or show them what climate change is doing to the earth. Others may be more compelled by the financial aspect of saving money, and others may like being more independent of government. At the end of the day, the motivation behind the change in behavior is irrelevant as long as the change occurs. Consider all the advantages of sustainable living every time you wonder why sustainable living is essential and desirable.

Sustainably Saves You Money and Is Not Expensive

In life, you rarely get anything for free. Sustainability will cost you a small price. If you look at it in the long term, the investments you make toward sustainability are small compared to the savings you'll make. Unfortunately, sustainable products and produce might be priced higher because environmental consideration is taken when creating them. For example, organic food grown without harmful pesticides will need more attention and labor to produce, which is often an added cost burden that the consumer feels. Things are frequently labeled organic when they are not, so always ensure you're not being taken advantage of by misleading packaging. However, sustainable living requires you to reduce food waste. If you can use everything you buy, you'll make fewer trips to the grocery store, saving you money on your food and transport bills. Organic food prices will not be problematic if you use your ingredients wisely.

Consumerism is rising, and it's easy to fall into the hype. You probably do not need a new phone every other year, but the standards in society may have convinced you that you do. If you are in the habit of thinking critically about your purchasing choices, you may reconsider and think, "If it works, I don't need a new one." Try to avoid buying for the sake of buying. Impulse buying can lead to you purchasing low-quality products with a short lifespan. Good quality appliances that are energy efficient will last longer and contribute to energy efficiency, ultimately saving you money.

Research any product that claims to be sustainable and verify its eco-friendly certification, if it has one. If you buy the correct item, it will save you money in the long term. For example, a hybrid vehicle is energy efficient because it uses a smaller energetic electric engine and regenerative braking to give you more miles on the road. Buying a hybrid or electric vehicle may cost you more upfront than buying a gas-only equivalent, but you will immediately benefit by getting more miles out of your gas tank. Now imagine these savings over many years or decades. This is what sustainable living affords you.

It's So Easy; You Can Start Today

Learning about sustainability can be overwhelming. You might go through a range of emotions, like shame, guilt, shock, or fear. You might wonder why you didn't know all these things or worry about how much harm you have done to the environment.

I don't want you to worry about the past or anything you used to do before you embarked on this journey. You should know that you don't have to do a green makeover all at once. This book is a guide with numerous steps, suggestions, and recommendations.

It is unlikely that you will be able to do everything the day you get started, and you should not feel pressured to do so. Sustainable living is a lifestyle that requires small, consistent efforts toward eco-friendly goals. Anything small you do counts and can make a big difference in your life. Give yourself ample time and patience, and give yourself a pat on the back for every change you make towards living a more sustainable lifestyle, big or small.

Here are some ways to start your sustainable living journey:

- Commit to recycling. Sort your waste to find out what can be recycled instead of just throwing your garbage in the trash.

- Ditch the single-use plastic water bottle for a reusable one.

- Install energy-efficient light bulbs, and switch off any lights and appliances that are not being used.

- Choose paperless billing at home and encourage it at your business.

- Start a garden, and see how much food you can grow.

- Use organic food waste to make your own compost.

- Minimize food waste in your household by not overcrowding food in your refrigerator and pantry. When you can easily view what is in your refrigerator and pantry, it's easy to see what you have or what is about to expire.

- Minimize water waste around your home by closing your taps tightly and fixing any leaks.

- You don't always have to buy new clothes; visit thrift and second-hand stores to find pre-loved fashions.

- Try to source local and organic food grown in your area. Eat what is in season, which will be freely available and cheap.

These small ways are how you can start living a sustainable life today without breaking the bank or breaking a sweat.

A Sustainable Mindset

Committing your mind, behavior, and habits to live a sustainable life means consciously aligning yourself with a sustainability mindset. You are deliberately divorcing yourself from how most people live their lives and trying to integrate yourself with your natural environment in a way that will cause the least damage.

Understand that sustainability permeates every aspect of your life and is holistic; it is less about quantity and more about quality. The idea is to do what you can for the environment now rather than wait for later. So many of our lifestyle habits go against nature and how it functions. Sustainability means trying to merge with nature and working with it and what it provides us. Sustainable living requires you to adjust your mind to think about long-term consequences and measure what your current actions will mean later. It's more than just looking at your lifetime; but at the lifetimes of those who will come along after you are gone.

Prepper's Mindset

Some people most knowledgeable about self-reliance and living a sustainable lifestyle would characterize themselves as preppers. A "prepper" is an individual who prepares for an event or eventuality. Merriam-Webster (Prepper, 2023) defines a prepper as "A person who gathers materials and makes plans in preparation for surviving a major disaster or cataclysm (such as worldwide economic collapse or war)."

The kind of prepper you are depends on what you focus on. Some people focus on a zero-waste lifestyle, while others focus on self-reliance and self-sustainability. Preppers include homesteaders and survivalists, who know a lot about living sustainably. The committed prepper adopts a preparedness lifestyle to insure against life's challenges, small and large (Akart, 2023). Arm yourself with the correct information by researching and gaining knowledge about a sustainable lifestyle.

Environmentalism vs. Conservationism

Environmentalism arose as a direct response to the abuse of the global environment. It deals with ethical, social, and political movements advocating for the protection of the environment and is a fairly new concept. Conservationism is similar to but also quite different from environmentalism. Conservationism mainly focuses on conserving natural resources, landmarks, and endangered species.

The difference between these two concepts regarding sustainability is that environmentalism is more political and concerned with things it is against; under this ideology, the environment must be saved from human abuse, set aside, and preserved. On the other hand, conservationism views the environment as something we use daily for survival, so we need to nurture and care for it. With conservationism, you are not just against things, but you're fighting for them, as well, the idea that fighting for sustainable living may lead to a better lifestyle for all.

You may have desired to lead a sustainable lifestyle for quite some time. It sounds like a vague concept; you may wonder what it means. There are various areas in your life that you can change to be more eco-friendly, including your mode of transport and even how you are buried. It is a whole lifestyle that you can tap into. If you read on, you'll find out what that entails in the following chapter. Knowledge is power. The more you know, the better your chances of implementing sustainable habits in your day-to-day life

2

A Sustainable Lifestyle

Your sustainable life includes aspects beyond your home, like the transportation you use. Traditional modes of transport rely heavily on the burning of fossil fuels. This is very detrimental to the environment as it increases CO2 emissions. In effect, global warming is speeding up, threatening the survival of many of the species on this earth, including humans. Switching to more sustainable modes of transport can help to slow down the effects of global warming.

Another example is the clothing industry which contributes to a lot of freshwater use and a consumerism mindset that results in a lot of waste. Learning to shop in thrift stores can teach us how to reuse clothing and other items. The chapter will also show you how to maintain a low-impact home and how you can even get buried in an eco-friendly way.

Sustainable Transportation .

The Benefits

There are numerous benefits associated with sustainable transport. Switching over to a sustainable mode of transport will reduce your carbon footprint and greenhouse gasses, noise, and air pollution (Collins, 2021). Sustainable transportation creates jobs as there is little to no existing infrastructure for green transportation. Employment in design, construction, engineering, maintenance, technology, and a number of other industries will be created, making it an inclusive form of job creation. Less pollution will be emitted via sustainable transportation and will positively affect the health of the community (Rinkesh, 2017).

People who choose public modes of transport contribute to less congestion than when each individual uses their own vehicle to transport themselves to and from work or school. When congestion is reduced, energy is saved, as there is less starting and stopping, which contributes to higher fuel consumption (Marsh, 2020).

When you purchase an electric vehicle or when infrastructure is built to accommodate sustainable public transportation, it can initially cost a lot of money. Over time, however, there are a ton of savings. You should consider eco-friendly commuting, be it a new electric vehicle, carpooling, or increasing your use of public transport. It may be different from what you are used to, but you may find you adapt quickly, enjoying the exercise of bike riding or having the time to read while someone else does the driving.

Types of Eco-Friendly Transport

To avoid modes of transport that are detrimental to the environment, you should know which modes of transport are green and don't harm the environment (or your wallet). Some of your sustainable options are listed below.

- Electric cars, trucks, and other large vehicles do not rely on fossil fuels; rather, they run on electricity. Maximize your sustainability by charging your electric vehicle with renewable energy like solar, wind, hydroelectric, and geothermal power.

- Electric motorcycles are becoming more common and can be charged using renewable energy, similar to the case of electric vehicles, as they typically also have a rechargeable battery. This type of transport has no emissions, and the cheapest model can cost you less than $10,000.

Electric vehicles are becoming more affordable every year.

- Electric bicycles, or e-bikes, have an electric motor and a rechargeable battery. The motor assists the rider by providing additional power when pedaling, allowing them to travel further and faster with less effort. E-bikes are often used for commuting, leisure, or as an alternative to traditional bicycles. They can come in various styles, including mountain, road, and city bikes. They can have different levels of motor assistance depending on the model. E-bikes are becoming increasingly popular as they provide an eco-friendly and efficient mode of transportation while providing exercise when wanted.

- Hydrogen vehicles are currently only found in California, the only state in the United States with a nexus of retail hydrogen fueling stations. This vehicle only emits water vapor, is quiet, and only takes around five minutes to refuel. Unfortunately, hydrogen fuel is not readily available, so you may have an issue refueling if you don't live in southern California.

- Multiple occupant vehicles or carpools reduce the number of cars on the road, reducing air pollution and CO2 emissions. Being in a carpool will also reduce the money you spend on transportation as you will share the fuel cost.

- Hybrid cars run on electricity generated by regenerative braking. This type of vehicle has lower greenhouse gas emissions compared to standard cars. You have to be careful about how you dispose of the substances contained in a hybrid car's battery, as they can harm the environment and contaminate the soil.

- Bicycles run on the power of your legs. There's no gas involved, and they do not plug into anything. You can use a bicycle to commute to and from work. A bike has no carbon emissions and is not detrimental to the environment.

- Walking is a no-brainer. As a sustainable form of transport, it requires no fossil fuels or energy costs. It is free and will improve your health if you walk more to get from point A to B. In fact, research has shown that walking can reduce your risk of dementia (Godman, 2022).

Lucky for you, there is more than one type of sustainable mode of transport. We have a variety of options to choose from, depending on your circumstances. If you cannot afford an electric vehicle, then perhaps you could carpool or use public transport. The choice is ultimately yours.

Hydrogen Cars

Hydrogen is an abundant gas element easily found in nature. Hydrogen vehicles run by taking in hydrogen from their tank and turning it into electricity that powers the motor, which propels the vehicle.

As hydrogen is burned along with oxygen, the only byproducts of a hydrogen tank and fuel cells are energy and water (Elstad, 2022).

This vehicle has no carbon emissions and does not contribute to global warming as it uses a clean fuel source. Refueling a hydrogen tank is required far less often than refilling a traditional gas tank. Therefore, drivers of hydrogen cars don't need to worry about locating hydrogen fuel stations often. Hydrogen cars are much lighter than regular cars and require less energy to propel them forward; in fact, they can accelerate more quickly than a typical car. However, as innovative as this vehicle is, it does come with a few disadvantages.

There are about 15,000 hydrogen-powered vehicles in the U.S. right now, and all of them are in California (Voelckler, 2022). Hydrogen vehicles need hydrogen fueling stations to function. Currently, California only has about 60 hydrogen fueling stations. Most of their hydrogen comes from a facility in Los Angeles that extracts it from Methane (Elstad, 2022). To make a hydrogen vehicle, there is a lot more use of rare metals for fuel cells, which places a burden on the environment due to the pollution that a hydrogen car-making plant produces. In short, some large-scale transportation companies are looking at hydrogen as an alternative, like container ships with predictable fueling stations. However, for smaller vehicles, it is unlikely it will become popular in the near future. Despite these restrictions, this is still one of the cleanest modes of transportation.

The Future of Sustainable Transport

Transportation supports numerous industries and makes global trade possible. Over two-thirds of global oil consumption is due to transportation (Swargari, 2021). The infrastructure of transport can result in harmful disruptions to ecosystems. To avoid air pollution and other adverse effects of fuel-burning vehicles on the environment, we should consider the green modes of transportation mentioned earlier in this chapter. Electric cars, public transit, carpools, bikes, and even unmanned aerial vehicles are where the future of transportation is taking us. You need to consider your individual capacity. Can you walk or cycle to your next location? Is there a mode of public transport or carpooling that you can take? You will also notice that the sustainable options are also the ones that are friendly to your wallet.

Thrift Shopping

Supporting the fast fashion industry can harm the environment. This is because making new clothes uses many natural resources and creates a lot of air and water pollution. By buying clothes from ethical brands or learning how to thrift shop, you can make more sustainable fashion choices.

Thrifting is purchasing pre-loved items at discounted prices. Because you are reusing an item, like clothing, for example, you are reducing the waste created in the production of a new one of that item. You are also reducing the waste that goes into a landfill. I have found that thrifting brings me great joy because I never know what I am going to find. So many fashion gems are hidden in thrift stores, just waiting for you to discover them.

Along with thrifting, there are also various strategies that you can use to save money while helping the environment. Use the following thrift store shopping strategies to gain super savings (Huffstetler, 2019, 9 thrift store shopping tips to save you money, n.d.).

- Use thrift store coupons to bring down bargain prices further.
- Check if the thrift store offers discounts that can maximize savings.
- Strategize and shop only when there is a sale.
- Dig in unsorted baskets for items that may not be priced.

- Look for clothing brands with lifetime warranties, like The North Face, Patagonia, or Eddie Bauer, that will repair zippers and tears for free.

- Shop at thrift outlet stores (like Goodwill) for cheap deals.

- Plan which items you will buy to avoid impulse buying and spending unnecessarily.

- Do not settle on items you don't love or that won't fit your style.

- Find thrift stores online to check for bargains.

- Don't buy what you don't need simply because the items are cheap.

When you enter a thrift store, remember to be in the right head-space so that you can patiently go through the different kinds of clothing (9 thrift shopping tips for saving money and the planet, 2023). Be sure about what you need and the budget you plan on spending. Remember to keep an open mind because you will come across torn and stained clothing that may put you off. You have to put in real effort to go through everything and ensure the item has all its hardware intact (zippers, buttons, snaps, etc.). Make sure the clothes do not have a foul odor, as some smells cannot be neutralized by laundry detergent and softener. Inspect the material and opt for natural fabrics like hemp, linen, wool, cotton, and leather.

The early bird catches the worm, so try to get to your thrift store bright and early so you can have the time, space, and freedom to comb through the stock thoroughly. Avoid the big thrift store chains and opt for smaller local thrift stores; it is even better if the charity thrift store you shop at aligns with a cause you believe in. The thrift store experience is unlike any other shopping experience, so make it your own. Put those earphones in, play some upbeat music, and get to bargain hunting!

Thrift Other Items

Clothes are one of many things that you can find at thrift stores. You can upcycle various items found at thrift stores; this can save you a lot of money in the long run and reduces the pollution caused by bringing your items to stores so that you can buy them. Here are a few things that you can purchase at thrift stores.

1. Furniture like dining tables, cabinets, chairs, and even cupboards can be found in good condition for under $100.

2. Dishes, especially vintage sets, are always a good deal when you find them. You can find vintage pottery items coveted in the thrifting world if you research and know how to recognize them.

3. Salt and pepper shakers usually go for less than $1 and can be upcycled into ornaments or decorations (25 nifty items you absolutely need to buy at thrift stores now, 2021). You can give them a fresh coat of paint if they are made of wood.

4. Artwork never gets old, and you can find plenty of pieces at a thrift store that are pleasing to the eye.

5. Mirrors are an exciting find as you can usually give them a makeover that will suit your taste.

6. You can purchase frames at thrift stores for their intended use. You can also think outside the box and turn them into bulletin boards, chalkboards, or decorations.

7. Children's clothing from thrift stores is usually in good condition because they only wear the clothes for a short time due to their fast-growing bodies.

8. Seasonal decorations are very affordable at thrift stores, and you can also spruce them up to make them look brand new. You can add new decorations to old wreaths for different seasons throughout the year.

9. I like to use vintage luggage to store photographs and keepsakes. They look cute, are easy to move about with the handles, and keep the bugs out.

There are a few items that wouldn't make sense to buy at a thrift store. Avoid purchasing a baby crib at a thrift store, as this may compromise the baby's safety due to weakened or loose parts that could become a choking hazard (Hisham, 2021). Once a helmet has sustained some impact due to a crash, its structure changes, and it can no longer effectively protect your head; do not buy a helmet at a thrift store. Stuffed animals can come with an infestation of pests that are not visible, so avoid them, too. Electrical appliances from thrift stores may have blunt blades, making their functioning more difficult. Underwear is an intimate item that should not be thrifted.

With all this advice, I'm sure you are now fully equipped to get started with your new sustainable fashion habit.

Can You Achieve a Low-Impact Home?

At some point, you may experience eco-anxiety that may make you feel helpless as you read what the future of the earth may look like if we carry on treating it like we currently are—it's going to take an immense effort to reverse what the human race has done to the environment. Even if the collective has not caught on, it doesn't mean that you should do nothing because your small efforts count.

Low-impact living is all about reducing your impact on the environment and earth's natural resources. It's a lifestyle that aims to lower your ecological footprint through daily actions and habits, from shopping locally to eating less meat to avoiding single-use plastics (Chelsea, 2020).

The way you travel and the kind of home you live in also influences your impact. It is the choices you make on a daily basis that will affect the environment the most. Low-impact living is possible because it is not a rigid set of rules; you get to make it what you can. Consider the choices you make, ask yourself how they will affect the environment, and then make informed eco-friendly decisions going forward. Refrain from trying to do everything at once, or you may end up doing nothing.

Burial Pods: Eco-Conscious Funerals

If you've had your eco-friendly ear to the ground, you may have come across the concept of tree pods or natural burials. Instead of being buried in a traditional coffin or being cremated and your ashes given to your family, a tree pod burial is a green alternative that saves money and improves the environment. A tree pod burial occurs when a biodegradable urn holding your cremated remains is buried. From that, a tree will grow that will be fed by your remains.

A tree pod burial promotes the idea that death is the only way you get to return to nature.

The Cost of a Tree Pod Burial

The average funeral in the United States costs between $7,000–$12,000 (Londen Insurance Group, Inc., 2023). This includes service fees, viewing of the deceased, burial, casket transportation, and other preparatory costs such as embalming. You may have to spend a little more on a tombstone and flowers.

You can save a lot of money if you choose a more biodegradable option, like a tree pod burial. The cost of cremation is around $1,100, and affordable biodegradable urns can cost less than $200 (Jacobson and Madden, 2023.). You can choose to get buried on your own property, depending on where you live (Wight, n.d.), or you can spend up to $4,000 to be buried in a conservation cemetery that protects your burial plot in perpetuity. As compared to traditional funerals, this may be a much cheaper option.

The Tree Pod Procedure

Once you have decided that a tree pod burial is suited to your needs, you will have to choose which tree will be planted when you die. On the actual day of your burial, the ashes are placed in the urn, closed, and buried. The tree you chose will then be planted above the earth, and your family and friends can care for it as it serves as your living memorial. After the burial, the urn will biodegrade, and the soil will be able to access your ashes for added nutrients.

Is This Burial for You?

Religions around the world dictate how a person should be buried. Strong cultural influences also dictate what should happen when a person dies. Having this kind of burial is very unconventional and non-traditional and may seem bizarre to people who have not considered such a burial. If you are intrigued by the idea of returning to nature and becoming one with the soil, tree pod burials may be proper for you, especially if you are eco-conscious. It is a way of leaving a living legacy that may still exist long after tombstones crumble.

How To Transition to Low-Impact Living

- Calculate your carbon footprint using a free online calculator that asks you questions about your transportation buying habits and energy use.

- Create a low-impact home by replacing plastic food containers with glass and silicone ones that can be reused numerous times. Use biodegradable products instead of plastic ones. Buy in bulk and pour your spices/coffee/grains/soap into refillable glass containers.

- Choose local products and buy from local stores, as you will be supporting your community without contributing to the environmental burden of transporting goods to places all over the earth.

- Check that products labeled organic, green, or sustainably sourced products have the proper certifications. Shop only where you trust that the labels are verified.

- Eating less commercially raised meat is healthy and advantageous to the environment. Regularly replace meat with plant-based proteins or carefully source your meat from local farmers, hunting, or fishing.

- Buy only what you need and minimize spending.

This kind of lifestyle can be peppered with sustainable choices so that you make a powerful impact, from the type of transportation you choose to the clothes you wear to the way you are buried when you leave this earth. Make like an electric car and get charged up because your journey is just beginning!

3

The 5 Rs

I grew up on the saying "reuse, reduce, recycle." This was primarily due to my mother's growing up during the depression and being very frugal. But as I became an adult, I began to appreciate the lessons she taught me, not only because, as a graduate student, I had no money but also because my interest in the environment was becoming a primary focus. Since then, the 3 R's has become the 5 R's. It wasn't until I was in my late twenties that I took the 5 R's to heart and started implementing them in my life. Despite my mother's thriftiness, growing up, my family produced a lot of waste. We were very careful to take care of things so they would last and not need replacing, and we rarely purchased things we didn't need; however, recycling in those days was far more complex. My parents were not gardeners either, so our bins were usually filled with plastic packaging, discarded processed food, organic waste, and other kinds of garbage. I always dreamed of living on a farm, and although that never happened, I knew that the way I was growing up was not the way I wanted to live once I got to run my own home. This chapter will guide you on how to try to achieve a zero-waste home through the 5 Rs. Not only will you learn tips on reducing your wastefulness, but you will also learn how to save money in the process.

Zero-Waste Lifestyle

Living a zero-waste lifestyle is living in such a way that you produce minimal waste. This includes reusing items around your home, recycling what you can, making a compost heap from organic matter, and refusing to use single-use packaging or items. There is much overlap between sustainable and zero-waste living. The main difference is that when people talk about zero-waste, they focus mainly on reducing trash. The zero-waste lifestyle focuses on using sustainable products made from biodegradable materials and limiting what is thrown away (Why sustainable living is so important, 2021).

Some of the habits needed for a zero-waste lifestyle will be explored further in the upcoming chapters of this book. For example;

- Instead of using disposable plastic or paper coffee cups, use a washable mug.
- Make your own cleaning products.
- Don't buy magazine after magazine; instead, read their online version.
- Buy items whose manufacturers allow for the return of the containers.
- Do not accept plastic bags; rather, bring your reusable shopping bags to carry your groceries.
- Choose sustainable toilet paper or a bidet, and avoid beauty products with plastic packaging.
- Use laundry products that have biodegradable packaging, and stop the use of disposable dryer sheets. Instead, opt for reusable wool dryer balls to reduce waste.

- You can probably benefit from consuming less food and buying less stuff. Before throwing something out, check if it may have a secondary use.

The 5 Rs

The 5 Rs outline a process of waste management that can drastically speed up your process of living in a zero-waste household. Understanding each step of this process and implementing each step correctly will lead you to a more sustainable lifestyle. The 5 Rs include refuse, reduce, reuse, recycle, and rot. The rest of this chapter explains each of the 5 Rs to give you better insight into this waste management process.

Refuse!

If you can prevent waste from entering your home, you can better control the amount of waste that comes from it. Refuse to take junk mail, promotional samples, and anything single-use. Somehow, you might find yourself collecting junk that you do not need, like plastic bags, business cards, flyers, samples, checks, gift bags, plastic straws, disposable cups, plastic toothbrushes, single-use drink bottles, and cotton buds. Refuse unnecessary items like straws in your drink, plastic packaging at the supermarket for fresh produce, or free samples for things you weren't planning to buy. It can be difficult to refuse, but once you start with the small stuff, you can build up from there.

Reduce!

Reducing waste is about getting clear about what you truly need and not purchasing for the sake of it. Reducing your consumption to only what is necessary will help the environment and save you money. You would be surprised at how little you can live on and still live a quality life. Here are some examples of easy ways to get started reducing:

- Invest in a reusable bottle or cup for takeaway beverages such as water or coffee to avoid purchasing disposable one-time-use cups.

- Keep your reusable grocery bags at the top of your grocery list or in the backseat of your vehicle so you don't forget them. Some grocery stores offer a 5¢ refund for those opting to forgo plastic bags.

- Take the time to scrutinize what you are buying and if the packaging is eco-friendly. Choose items that come without much packaging, or at the very least, packaging that can be recycled and buy in bulk.

- Go paperless for your billing.

Rot!

Rotting your organic waste allows you to transform it into nutrients you can return to the soil. You can compost your organic waste in different ways, like having a garden compost, vermicomposting, or the Bokashi method (Vanderlinden, 2022). Compost is defined as organic matter that has been decomposed, such as leaves, kitchen scraps, grass, and organic waste from gardening. Certain microorganisms, fungi, and earthworms help your compost break down and create a dark compost that serves as a fertilizer rich in nutrients. Composting makes your soil fertile and your plants healthier. You can save money because you don't need to buy expensive artificial fertilizers, and it helps to balance the pH levels in your soil. Below are some of the items you can rot (Batista, 2020)

Compostable kitchen items include:

- Old bread or crumbs

- Fruits and Vegetables

- Previously-used brown paper bags and napkins

- Corn cob remains

- Dried herbs and spices that have gone stale

- Toothpicks and anything wooden

- Dried legumes that are old

- Cardboard (uncoated, small pieces)

- Coffer grounds and filters

- Eggshells

- Fireplace ashes (from natural wood only)

- Nutshells

- Compostable garden items consist of the following:

- leftover or unused garden soil

- dead leaves and plants

- pine needles and cones

- bush trimmings

- ash from wood

- Grass Clippings

- Hay and straw

- Hair and fur

- uncoated rope and twine

- tiny sticks and twigs

There are different types of compost that you can get started with. A compost pile consists of green and brown matter from your home mixed with some soil that you turn every once in a while to aerate. You can prevent odor by mixing two to three parts carbon-heavy "browns" for every one part nitrogen-centric "greens" (Mackenzie, 2016). You can put your compost pile in the corner of your garden.

Alternatively, you may purchase a large compost bin or build your own. A compost tumbler is a large bin with a wheel you can spin to mix up your compost material. You can take your organic material straight to your compost bin.

The third type of composting is kitchen composting, where you keep a small bin for the organic matter under the sink or on the kitchen counter. You can even use red worms in a bin to compost indoors if you live in an apartment (Mackenzie, 2016).

Avoid composting the following:

1. Charcoal or coal and its ashes may contain harmful substances to plants and soil.

2. Pet waste can contain bacteria, parasites, and pathogens harmful to humans.

3. Dairy products and eggs should not be added to the compost heap as they will produce a foul smell as they decompose and attract unwanted pests.

4. Any fat, lard, or grease will also generate an odor and attract pests.

5. Fish and meat scraps should not be added to your compost pile as they may contain bacteria and will also attract pests and small critters.

6. Do not try to add any plastic or inorganic materials, as they will not decompose.

An exception from the above list is meat and dairy used in Bokashi composting. The Bokashi method of composting does allow you to add meat and dairy. This method requires special equipment and uses fermentation as part of the process. This method only takes about ten days to convert organic matter into usable material and provides some of the highest nutrient value of any form of composting (Vanderlinden, 2022).

If your compost heap needs some nitrogen, add some grass clippings for a boost. Remember to shred your newspaper or plain white paper to speed up its decomposition when it hits the compost pile (Tips and tricks, 2023). Coffee grounds in your compost pile can help to attract worms who love the stuff. If any of your plants have any pesticides, do not add them to the pile.

If you want to know if your compost is ready, you will notice that it has halved in size but is much denser. Aerate your pile often to avoid any foul smells. Starting your own compost pile is as easy as getting your organic kitchen scraps, throwing them in one location, and turning the pile ever so often.

Recycle!

The world's population has reached a point where it consumes more than it can recycle. This means much waste is compacted into landfills or disposed of in incineration plants. Additionally, America tends to ship its recycling overseas, increasing its carbon footprint (14 Easy Ways to Start Living a Zero Waste Lifestyle, 2022). It is crucial that before you get to the recycling phase, you refuse waste and reduce your consumption.

To recycle is to return a product to its previous state in the production cycle. This means it will turn back into a raw material that can be used to make something else. The first step of recycling is to separate your waste into different categories, such as plastic, glass, metal, electronics, and organic waste. Recycling is vital as it conserves resources while reducing pollution. If more things are recycled, there is less need to cut down trees or mine for more minerals and raw materials. The more objects that are recycled, the slower the landfills fill up.

Avoid putting plastic bags in your recycle pile; take them to specific drop-off points for recycling plastic instead. If your plastic grocery bags end up in the garbage, they can be a hazard for animals and will contribute to a breakdown in machinery. Do not bundle your recyclable material in a plastic bag, as it will be considered trash (7 tips to recycle better, 2022).

There are different kinds of plastics; you should know the difference because some are more recyclable than others. Rigid plastics are classified by resin codes 1–7. The higher the resin code, the harder it is to recycle that kind of plastic. For example, resin codes 1–2 plastics are easy to recycle and have a higher value (The Nature Conservancy, 2018), whereas resin codes 3–7 might prove more difficult. The rules governing what kind of plastic can be recycled can get confusing, but once you get the hang of it, it will be like second nature. Don't be afraid to ask questions at your local recycling center.

Wish cycling occurs when you include non-recyclable items in recycling bins. Non-recyclable items act like a contaminant when they are among recyclable objects. In this case, the whole batch could end up in a landfill instead of being recycled. It is better not to include an object if you don't know what it is made of.

So, what can you recycle?

- Plastics with resin codes 1 and 2 can be recycled. Check the triangle recycling symbol beneath the container to see its classification. Plastic bottles, jugs, and tubs are examples of these recyclable materials. Don't forget that they should be empty and rinsed.

- Glass bottles and jars can be recycled. They, too, should be emptied and rinsed out to be ready for recycling. Do not include kitchen or window glassware, as they may have certain chemicals or additives that will contaminate other recyclable materials.

- Aluminum is also readily recycled, with the exception of aluminum foil that has food waste on it. To avoid contamination, wash out and empty the aluminum.

- Plain paper products like printer paper, magazine paper, cardboard rolls, and boxes, or your mail can be recycled. Anything with food waste or oil on it, like paper towels or pizza boxes, should not be included as they will lead to contamination.

Get different bins for different items and label them accordingly. Write down the local recycling rules somewhere visible so your household understands what is going on and can adhere to them easily. Before handing over your recyclable materials to the recycling plant, check for items that could potentially render the batch trash and remove them. Remember to use the other Rs, as recycling is often the last option for reducing waste, and recycling is less environmentally effective than proactively curbing waste (MasterClass, 2021).

Reuse!

Reuse involves extending the lifespan of an object. Reusing items requires you to think about different ways you can use them before throwing them out. I like "reuse" the most out of all the Rs because it requires maximizing your creativity. You can use a single item over many years, repurposing it and changing how it benefits your life. By reusing an item, you are breathing new life into something that could have been headed to a landfill.

Reuse means to use again and to find a new use for something instead of buying a new item to fulfill your need. If you can't think of a secondary use for an object, you can donate it to someone else, be it a loved one or a local charity. To make some extra money on the side, you can sell your old items on an online marketplace like Facebook or eBay or have a garage sale. Reusing things can also save you money as it delays you going out and buying new stuff.

Repurposing is a way to reuse things. Unlike reusing items, when you repurpose them, the secondary differs from what the item was used for initially. For example, toothbrushes can become cleaning brushes, and glass jars can hold homemade jams and preserves. You can save money if you reuse more and purchase less.

Here are some ideas of items that can be reused numerous times:

- Glass containers and jars can be reused to hold pantry items like grains, cereals, and other bulk buys. They can also be used as a desk or bathroom organizer. I have a number of them organizing my nails, bolts, and screws. Their reuse potential goes beyond food.

- Magazines and newspapers can be taken to your local doctor or dentist's office. You can make your own envelopes or paper mâché ornaments. Paper is a versatile material to work with, and what you can make with it is limited only by your imagination.

- Towels and clothes do not need to be thrown out. If they can be cut up to make napkins or cleaning rags, do that. One creative idea is to turn your old clothes into woven or braided rugs (Baker 2019). If you have sewing skills, you can take your reusing to a new level, sew quilts for loved ones, or make new clothes from old ones. I make draft blockers for my doors.

- Old furniture can be repaired or given a new finish rather than getting thrown out. If it is broken, you can repair it or break it down into smaller pieces, like shelves or shadow boxes.

- Plastic bags can be reused to line your trash bin or as grocery store carriers. You can reuse them to weave grocery tote bags. The inner plastic bag that carries cereal can be reused after rinsing to serve as sandwich wraps.

- Food scraps composed of organic material can be added to a compost bin.

- Egg cartons can be reused as a paint palette, a seedling starter, or an organizer for nuts and bolts. You can also donate your egg cartons to local egg producers so they don't have to buy new ones.

- Used tea bags are great at reducing the puffiness around your eyes and can help relieve skin irritation from insect bites or minor burns. (Remember to cool them first!) You can also dump the contents of the tea bag directly onto your topsoil to rejuvenate your flowers and plants (Ashley, 2014).

You can transform yourself into a handyperson by repairing items such as electronics, furniture, and clothes. If you don't deem yourself handy, you can enlist the services of a local repair person. Make sure to reuse any stationery items and utilize waste paper to take notes. Find other uses for excess rubber bands, paper clips, or folders that are lying around (Peach, 2023). Instead of rushing out to buy items, see if someone you know has what you need and borrow it; if you can rent something or share it, try that instead of purchasing outright. Remember that if you cannot find a secondary use for an object in your home, someone else may have a better need and use for it. Donate what you can to charity and sell the rest.

By using the 5 Rs of waste management, you can effectively take control of the waste you produce. Do not feel pressured to do everything at once. Start with one R, perfect it, and then move on to the next R. Indeed, some people now believe there is a 6th R that may be the most important and should come first, "Rethink." Rethink means being more mindful of your consumption habits and asking yourself, "Do I really need that?" (Rinalducci, 2023). By harmonizing the 5 Rs, you can save a lot of money and buy a lot less stuff. Buying less means less junk in landfills, which is better for our planet.

The following chapter focuses on do-it-yourself (DIY) and how it can save you money while keeping your habits eco-friendly. So, get to making a belt from watches—you might find it's not a complete "waist" of time.

4

Sustainability Through DIY

Today's world consumes a lot. A few centuries ago, people made most things at home (even their clothes), whereas people today buy many things. Be it gadgets, clothing, food, or cleaning chemicals, the current generation has gotten used to buying everything.

But what if you didn't have to? What if you could find a way to be more sustainable by doing more do-it-yourself (DIY) projects and buying less? There are many ways you can wield the power of DIY; some people can even make a business out of it.

For example, take Stephanie Seferian, who founded Mama Minimalist, a business that helps families all around the world start an eco-conscious life that simplifies sustainability. She believes using DIY can reduce the amount of trash your home produces, especially by upcycling goods in your home. Glass jars can become beeswax candles, and clothing material can become handkerchiefs, napkins, and so many other things. Stephanie advises that the best way to tackle DIY projects is to have goals for the short term and goals for the long term.

Simon Henson, who runs Best Sports Lounge (which focuses on getting fit by exploring lesser-known sports), uses DIY to bond with his children. As a father, Simon wanted to show his kids the various DIY skills he learned and ensure they understood that they should be economically, socially, and environmentally aware of their responsibility to the Earth. Simon feels DIY teaches his children the value of hard work while being engaging and exciting; he wants to set the right example.

Stephanie and Simon have dedicated their lives to saving money through various DIY products, and you can live the same way. This chapter will explain what DIY products can make your home more sustainable.

DIY and Save!

Taking on DIY projects can have the same sustainable effect as green upgrades to your energy supply. Luckily, DIY costs little to implement compared to installing a solar power system, for example. By doing what you can, you can save money while ensuring your home is more sustainable.

Be Your Own Maintenance Person

If you take the time to ensure that everything in your home is working as it should, you can avoid waste and high energy bills. Ensure that no faucets are leaking or dripping water; if your washer connection leaks, fix it by tightening the connection to the tap. Make sure that dust does not settle inside or outside your appliances, as this may cause them to need more power during use (Green Journal, 2018). Check that no air leaks are coming in from your windows or doors. An airtight home makes heating and cooling much easier for your heating, ventilation, and air conditioning (HVAC) system, thus reducing the financial burden on your energy bill. Applying weatherstripping, insulating drapes, and cloth draft stoppers (which you can make with left-over material) can make your doors and windows airtight.

Replace What You Can

Toilet fixtures and shower heads that are water efficient can help you save money on your utility bill. Using less water goes a long way in making your home more eco-friendly. Ensure that your light bulbs are energy efficient (like CFLs or LEDs). Lighting accounts for 12% of the electricity consumed around the globe each year (Weinert, 2022). Replacing all your light bulbs may be a bit pricey initially, but the energy-efficient ones are changed much less frequently while saving money on your energy bill because they use less power. You can also replace using your tumble dryer with a clothesline in the summer so that your clothes dry in the sunlight instead.

Rainwater Harvesting

You can build a rainwater harvesting system to take advantage of the water that comes from rain. You can use the collected water to water your flowers or vegetable garden or to wash your car. Instead of purchasing a rainwater harvesting system, you can build your own and customize it to your home. Installing a rain gutter around your roof leading to a water barrel/reservoir will catch rainwater you can use in and around your home. It also can have the added benefit of preventing water from damaging your home's foundation (Peterson, 2016).

Grow Your Food

You don't have to buy all your fruit and vegetables at a supermarket. You may be unable to determine what fertilizers and chemicals were put on the fresh produce you buy. So many harmful emissions occur in commercial food production, contributing to soil and water pollution. To help lessen the load on the environment and your wallet, it is better that you grow your food at home or shop at local farmers' markets.

When you start your own vegetable garden, you have control over the kind of pesticides and fertilizers you use. You will also feel a sense of accomplishment that you could take something from a seed and grow it into food. If a vegetable garden sounds intimidating, you can start with easy-to-grow herbs like parsley and basil indoors.

Make Your Own Cleaning Products

Most households have a cleaning product for everything, from the floors and the windows to the cutlery and crockery. This marketing scheme has resulted in numerous homes worldwide having harmful chemicals in the cupboards under the guise of keeping a clean house. You can make your own cleaning products that are safe and free of toxic chemicals instead.

For example, mixing baking soda with vinegar can create a powerful cleaning agent that can clean stainless steel, whiten bathroom tiles, and clean stains on the carpet and the inside of your refrigerator. If you have family members with eczema or asthma, they might benefit from using a cleaning agent that does not exacerbate their allergies.

Create Your Own Beauty Products

Did you know that you can make your own shampoo or deodorant? By having complete control over what ingredients go into your personal care products, you can up the ante on your level of sustainability. For example, deodorant can be made from high-proof liquor and tea tree essential oil, and shampoo can be made from baking soda and water.

There are no strict regulations on the ingredients that can be added to cosmetic products; therefore, you might be harming the environment and your family by buying what's available on the shelf at the store. When you make your beauty products, you save money and cut out toxic ingredients. Making your own beauty products also allows you to upcycle any containers, thus reducing waste.

Mow Your Own Lawn and Remove Your Own Snow

Instead of spending money on a landscaping company or lawn care service, you can purchase a lawn mower and mow it yourself. Excellent electric lawnmowers are available now. You can even cost-share the lawn mower purchase with your neighbors or family members and create a roster for who uses it and when (17 simple home DIY projects that will save you money, 2019). Better yet, look into clover lawn that requires less mowing and watering but attracts pollinators (Lovely, 2022).

You can also remove snow and ice from your walkways and porch. You do not need to pay for this service or use machines contributing to CO_2 emissions. By simply using your shovel to remove snow, you can help the environment while enjoying the total body workout.

Make Your Own Yogurt

Yogurt is not complicated to make, and you can make your own delicious batches at home. Most yogurt containers are #5, making them non-recyclable, so by making your own yogurt, you are enjoying a fresher product and reducing plastic waste. You can even use coconut milk to make yogurt if you are lactose intolerant. Whether starting the recipe from scratch or using a yogurt starter, it takes a minimum of eight hours after mixing all the ingredients to have your own yogurt. Alternatively, you can purchase a yogurt maker and use it only when making large batches (to save power).

Kickstart Your DIY Journey
With These Easy Projects

When it comes to specific DIY projects, you may not know exactly where to start. As with everything else, practice makes perfect, so do not be discouraged if your first DIY project feels like an epic fail. Always follow instructions and keep on trying. The following suggestions will make your home more eco-friendly and bring a new level of sustainability to how your home functions (Bueno, 2022).

Make a Drying Rack for Your Clothes

If you are cutting down the use of your tumble dryer, you will need somewhere to dry your clothes. You may not have access to a clothesline outside, so you might want to make a clothes-drying rack. This project is easy if you have repurposed wood, an old broomstick, or a wooden pole. You can make it a permanent fixture by nailing it to your patio or balcony wall. Put the rods on hinges so they can swing out of the way when not in use. Your drying rack can also be a temporary fixture by placing a broomstick on the backs of two opposite-facing chairs.

Make a Compost Bin

Making a compost bin is an excellent way to repurpose food waste that can greatly benefit your garden. Your garbage will no longer fill up with organic material, as you will instead be using food scraps to create compost for your flower beds and vegetable patch. In this way, your soil will benefit as you replenish its physical, chemical, and biological properties with your own organic compost. Composting will lessen the need for you to purchase harmful pesticides and fertilizers. Instead of buying a compost bin from your local hardware store, you can easily create it independently. Repurposing large plastic containers by drilling a few small holes (for aeration) is one way to make a compost bin.

Make Yourself a Plant Stand

Filling your home with indoor plants can drastically increase indoor air quality. Bamboo palms, English ivy, and Chinese evergreens are examples of plants that act as filters, cleaning the air so that you can breathe better air free from toxic pollutants (Garrity and Gautieri, 2023). Wanting indoor plants is common, but do you have the space? You can create a plant stand if your home does not have enough space to scatter the plants on various surfaces. It is easy to find designs online on how to create a multi-tiered plant stand. You may not even have to find material elsewhere as you can use old cabinets or tables to make your plant stand. While taking up only a little space, it can accommodate numerous plants for maximum impact on the air quality in your home.

Create an Ottoman Toy Box

Instead of purchasing large plastic containers to store toys, you can reuse old wooden furniture and clothes to create an ottoman toy box. You might need to buy a few extra supplies, but you can find all the required materials within your home or at a thrift store. You can cut up various clothes to create a pattern covering the ottoman. This way, toys usually strewn about can be stored in a neat and stylish container. If you make an ottoman using a trunk or another type of box, ensure the closing mechanism is child safe.

Put Together a Rain Collection System

If you desire to harvest rainwater, having a rain barrel can help you store it for later use. Relying more on rainwater can help ease the burden we place on freshwater resources. Regular rain barrels can be anywhere from 30–100 gallons, usually made from plastic. If you are unable to purchase rain barrels, you can upcycle any large containers you have lying around the house, as long as they do not contain any toxic liquids or chemicals. Avoid using wood or tin as water usually erodes both types of material.

DIY Beauty

There are so many benefits that come with making your own beauty products. Beauty products are often found in harmful plastic containers and are transported from all around the world using fuel-burning vehicles. When you make your own beauty products, you reduce the amount of plastic used in your home and CO2 emissions. Also, when you purchase beauty products from the store, they can be surprisingly expensive for tiny amounts. That requires you to purchase products with those containers repeatedly. You may find that when you make your own beauty products, you spend a lot less.

Certain ingredients found in commercial beauty products can lead to cancer, hormonal imbalances, and allergies (Mama Minimalist, 2018). Ingredients like BHA and BHT, aluminum, and triclosan are known to harm your health but can still be found in certain personal care products. When you DIY your beauty products, you have control over the ingredients you put in them and can avoid including harmful chemicals or substances that can negatively affect your health. This section will help you to make your own makeup, skincare, and hair care products.

DIY Makeup

Use the following simple recipes to make your own makeup.

- Creating your own lip balm is as easy as mixing coconut oil, beeswax, and cocoa butter. You only need three tablespoons of coconut oil, one-quarter cup of grated beeswax, one tablespoon of almond oil, and two tablespoons of cocoa butter. If any ingredients are solid, melt them in the microwave for 15 seconds, then mix them all while warm. Pour the mixture into lip balm containers and allow them to cool. Once cooled, the lip balm can be applied to the lips when needed.

- Mascara can be made from four teaspoons of aloe vera, two teaspoons of coconut oil, and one teaspoon of grated beeswax. Melt all of the ingredients in a small saucepan on low heat. To make the mascara black, add half a teaspoon of activated charcoal or half a teaspoon of cocoa powder for brown. Mix well and transfer to a mascara container.

- Eyeshadow is simple to make if you have one teaspoon of eye shadow pigment and a few drops of isopropyl alcohol. Apply pressure and press the eyeshadow paste with a dry paper towel. Alternatively, you can use the pigments as a loose powder.

DIY Skin Care

You can create a skincare routine with products that consist of only organic and safe ingredients. Make your own skincare products by following these easy steps (Barcal, 2022).

- Create your own body wash using equal parts coconut oil, honey, and Castile soap. Stir all ingredients until thoroughly mixed, then pour into a glass jar or plastic container. Use any essential oil to add your preferred fragrance; you can add 10–15 drops of lavender, orange, or chamomile.

- Olive oil can be used as a body oil. If you combine it with a few drops of chamomile, your body oil can have anti-aging properties that give dry skin a boost of moisture. Tea tree oil has anti-inflammatory properties, while cedarwood oil also can reduce skin irritations. Fragrant essential oils such as lavender, clary sage, and peppermint can give your body oil a pleasant scent.

- If you mix equal parts of sugar and an oil of your choice (olive or coconut), you can make an effective and easy-to-use body scrub. Store in a cool place in a small container. If you want to make it smell nice, you may mix in half a teaspoon of vanilla extract.

- You can make a facial mask with several ingredients in your kitchen. Mixing egg whites with turmeric and orange juice can help to minimize the pores on your face, while honey, raw oats, and mashed banana reduce the redness in your skin. Half an avocado combined with one tablespoon of yogurt and one tablespoon of honey creates a mask that can moisturize the skin. Lastly, you can mix lemon, cinnamon, and honey for a face mask that calms the skin.

DIY Hair Care

You can mix a variety of ingredients to create eco-friendly hair care products.

- If you combine equal parts Castile soap and water, you get a simple shampoo that you can use to cleanse your hair. By adding olive oil, you can make it moisturizing, while drops of essential oils can add a pleasant scent.

- Mixing aloe vera gel and drops of essential oil can create a pleasant-smelling hair gel. It keeps for around three months at room temperature in an airtight container.

- Mixing one avocado or mashed banana, four ounces of full-fat plain yogurt, one teaspoon of honey, and one teaspoon of olive oil or coconut oil can give you a moisturizing conditioner that can be stored in the fridge for up to a week. Apply to the hair after shampooing and allow it to sit for three to five minutes before washing it out thoroughly.

- Hairspray can be made by mixing one teaspoon of gelatin with eight ounces of hot water. Stir the mixture until the gelatin is dissolved. Once cooled, you can transfer the mixture to a spray bottle and use it as needed. This organic hair spray can be kept at room temperature for about half a year but may need to be shaken before use as the ingredients can separate occasionally.

Mixing easily obtainable, organic, and affordable ingredients allows you to switch to more sustainable DIY beauty products that ensure you still feel good about yourself. Not only will you save money, but you will also reduce the amount of waste and plastic in your home. The harmful chemicals found in cosmetic products that may affect your health will also be a thing of the past.

DIY Cleaning Products

There are so many toxic chemicals in cleaning products. Switching to a more eco-friendly option, like making your cleaners, can improve indoor air quality and your health. The indoor air pollutants in commercial cleaning products can cause fatigue, dizziness, headaches, allergies that affect the nose, eyes, and throat, and even heart disease, respiratory complications, and cancer.

Cleaning products contain acids, bases, salts, phosphates, solvents, surfactants, fragrances, and glycol ethers. These chemicals may disrupt your hormone functions and cause skin and lung disorders. DIY cleaners will not have any of these harmful ingredients, yet they clean just as well. Here are some easy recipes from Hubbard (2022) for different types of cleaners that you can use around the house that are eco-friendly, affordable, and won't negatively affect your health.

All-Purpose General Cleaner

This general cleaner can be used on most surfaces except aluminum, cast iron, natural stone, or anything with wax.

What you will need:

- Mason jar, preferred quart-sized

- peels of any citrus fruit

- distilled white vinegar

- 1 tsp Castile soap

- 1 cup water

- spray bottle

Place all your citrus peels into your mason jar and fill it with distilled vinegar to the brim. Shut tightly. Allow this mixture to infuse over a couple of weeks, where it can receive a lot of sunlight. Strain the vinegar, pour half a cup into a spray bottle, then add your water and Castile soap. Shake well and use with a cloth.

Vinegar-Free Cleaner

Your cleaner does not always have to include vinegar. If you don't want to use it, you can make a cleaner that is vinegar free by mixing two cups of water with one tablespoon of unscented liquid Castile soap. Pour this into a spray bottle, and you can get to cleaning immediately.

Borax-Free Laundry Detergent

This DIY laundry detergent recipe is machine safe and works effectively despite containing no Borax.

What you will need:

- a big jug

- 35–40 drops of essential oil of your choice

- 1 cup salt

- 1 cup washing soda

- 1 cup baking soda

- 1.5 cups unscented liquid Castile soap

Mix the baking soda, washing soda, and salt. Add the liquid Castile soap and essential oils and continue to mix until well combined.

Grout Cleaner

Use this cleaner with a toothbrush, and it will give your tiled surfaces a new shine.

What you will need:

- 0.5 cup of baking soda
- 0.25 cup hydrogen peroxide
- 1 tsp dish soap

Mix all the ingredients and apply. After 5-10 minutes, scrub and rinse.

Wood Cleaner

Nourish and clean your wood surfaces with olive oil.

What you will need:

- 0.25 cup lemon juice
- 0.5 cup of olive oil

Combine ingredients and apply with a soft cloth.

The interesting thing about DIY cleaners is that you can make the most of them with a bit of creativity. There are numerous safe ingredients at your disposal that you can use to make your cleaning products.

If you are ever looking for DIY inspiration, the "Spoonflower Blog" or the "Make Use Of" websites have some nifty ideas for things you can make with little to no expertise. Making your own products and doing your own repairs and replacements can ease the load on the environment and save you some money.

It can be challenging to begin DIYing when you are used to the convenience of relying on quick solutions. Fortunately, the more you do something, the better you get at it. Do not be discouraged by any DIY fails that come your way; use failure as a stepping stone to get better at what you are attempting. DIY is all about learning and trying new things. Have fun with it! The next chapter will explore the idea of backyard farming and gardening in cities. Use the steps in the next chapter to advance your sustainability journey.

5

Going and Growing Green in Cities

Imagine bending down to pick some ripe bell peppers or clipping off fresh rosemary from your backyard or balcony. What if you could snip off your cherry tomatoes from their vine and walk into your kitchen, wash them, and add them to a salad you are preparing for your family? There is some satisfaction in tilling the soil and watching your food go from being a tiny seed filled with potential to a plant that can nourish your body.

Backyard gardening is gaining popularity because people are not satisfied with the quality of the food available in stores. This movement resonated because I enjoy fresh organic produce packed with nutrients. The price tag that comes with buying organic can sometimes be steep, and it also drove me to experiment with backyard gardening. Once I started, I could not stop. My family and friends also enjoy the excess vegetables I give away when I have an abundant harvest.

Whether you live in a home with a backyard or a small one-bedroom apartment, you can take advantage of growing your own food. Vertical gardening, for example, makes growing food in small spaces easy, so anything is possible. A backyard garden will provide your family with food and reduce the area your lawn takes. It doesn't matter what you start with; just start.

In addition to growing your own food, if you do have a yard, you could try rearing small animals like chickens or miniature goats. You may not be able to fit a cow in a small space, but chickens can be kept in a small yard. You can check with your local zoning office for their ordinances on the regulations of keeping chickens in your backyard (State laws concerning backyard chickens, n.d.). If you are really ambitious, you can contemplate the idea of beekeeping. You may be able to lease space in open areas for your boxes if you do not have appropriate space at home. The global bee population is in decline, and your community could benefit from a colony of honey bees. You will enjoy not only the honey but also the beeswax, as it can be included in numerous homemade lotion recipes. This chapter will guide you as you explore backyard farming, beekeeping, pollinator gardening, and organic pest control for sustainability while saving money in the process. Let's get buzzing!

Backyard Income

Investing in urban agricultural activities can boost your home's sustainability and make you extra cash. You can quickly turn a hobby you enjoy into a money-making prospect. The following activities can help you generate some income while having fun doing some backyard agriculture.

Sell Your Homemade Compost

Compost returns the nutrients back into your soil and improves its overall health. You can make some money by producing large amounts of compost and selling it. Not all gardeners are fond of making their own compost heap, but they still need to add compost to their garden soil.

Sell Your Produce

Any excess fruits, vegetables, or herbs from your backyard garden can be sold to others for profit. So instead of preserving a lot of your produce or giving it away, you can sell it to your neighbors or loved ones. People need to eat every day, so you will always have hungry customers.

Sell Your Eggs

Around 15 hens give you almost a dozen eggs daily, which is a lot for a family of four to consume. Any excess eggs can be sold, so you can quickly see a return on investment. People don't have to get their eggs from the farmers' market or the grocery store, as you can easily provide for your neighbors, family, and friends by keeping hens. Recent bird flu epidemics have caused the price of eggs to skyrocket in the U.S. It is possible that the virus, which currently is sporadic and seasonal, will become endemic, and prices will remain high (Aubrey, 2023).

Chickens love when the garden soil is being prepped by rototilling.

Sell Your Seedlings

Getting started with seedlings is fun, and sometimes you can sprout too many. You can sell off any extra seedlings you have. It takes little extra care or work to get them started on a large scale, and they're easy to sell on Facebook or at your local farmer's market. Seedling sales may not make you a millionaire, but they can help you make extra money to purchase small items for your garden.

Sell Your Herbs

Growing herbs in your garden allows you to sell them fresh or dry them and sell dried herbs. Depending on where you plant them, they can grow like weeds. They are cheap to produce and won't require too much maintenance. Herbs are always in high demand but can be pretty pricey to purchase. You can offer a more affordable alternative to your community by selling them your herbs.

Swap Meet

You can swap produce with another farmer if you have too much of one thing. For example, if you have too much basil, you can swap it for some thyme or mint. What you get in the trade will depend on whom you are swapping with, so check with your local farmers to see if anyone is interested in what you have and if you're interested in what they have.

Getting Started

To get started with backyard gardening, you need to collect information regarding certain aspects of it, like the placement of your garden, what you can grow, the climate you live in, and so forth. Arming yourself with the correct information will help you prepare adequately for a successful harvest. There are various factors that you must consider that will influence your results.

1. Check what your local weather patterns are. Is your region's climate hot, dry, cold, or wet? Depending on your climate, you can only plant things that thrive in your region. If weeds are growing freely in your locality, you will likely be able to grow vegetables.

2. Check local nurseries or stores for discounted offers on backyard gardening supplies. Look around for any discounts on fertilizer manure, fruit trees, or seeds, especially toward the end of the growing season. Some municipalities offer their constituents soil, mulch, and wood chips at lower prices than commercially available (Worst, 2020). Speak to your neighbors and see what they may have growing in their gardens, as they will likely grow well in your garden, too.

3. You will need to organize your backyard garden to grow certain things in certain places. Farmers usually grow one crop in a straight line, but you do not need to follow this procedure as you may not have enough space. If you have the proper spacing between each plant, you can put your plants in whatever order you wish. Place your backyard garden close to a water source so you can easily water it. Don't make your plots or rows too big, or you will be tempted to walk through them, compacting the ground (Neverman, 2021).

4. Where you decide to plant your crops will be dictated by the layout of your home. Prioritize perennial plants and trees, as they will be permanent fixtures in your garden. After figuring out where to place your perennials and trees, you can focus on annual crops that only grow during a specific season. Use a pen and paper to draw it out and plan what you will put where.

5. Consider the possible wildlife that may be attracted to your garden. Deer and rabbits like fresh organic vegetables too. Prepare proper fencing or use non-toxic repellents (Neverman, 2020).

6. Choosing what to grow will be determined by your family's needs and what grows easily in your region. Sweet potatoes and beans are good sources of macronutrients, while nut trees produce nuts packed with fats and proteins. Fruits and vegetables can cost the most in any grocery store, so these are high-value products that you will want to include in your backyard farming. You may not be able to plant enough so that your house becomes self-sufficient in growing its own fruits and vegetables, but any contribution will benefit your health and your pocketbook.

Prepping the Soil

The soil in your backyard should not just be dirt from the ground. You have to keep adding nutrients to it so it can pass those nutrients to the plant. You must check what kind of soil you have and what would thrive in it. Below are the six common soil types and what grows best in them (Barton, 2013)

- Clay soil retains a lot of water and has few air pockets, but if the drainage is enhanced, it is suitable for growing fruit trees, summer vegetables, and shrubs.

- Sandy soil is easy to cultivate and dries out quite quickly. You may need to supplement it with organic fertilizer, but it will allow crops like carrots, potatoes, and parsnips to thrive, as well as strawberries, corn, lettuce, tomatoes, and collard greens.

- Silty soil is good for most fruit and vegetable crops, provided sufficient drainage exists. This type of soil feels soft and holds moisture well.

- Peaty soil often feels moist as it has a high level of peat; with enough drainage, it can support the growth of crops like legumes, root vegetables, and leafy greens.

- Chalky soil contains stones and may have elements of chalk or limestone. It drains efficiently, and vegetables like sweet corn, cabbage, beets, and spinach thrive in it.

- Loamy soil is a healthy mix of silt, sand, and clay soil and is the best soil for backyard gardening. Loamy soil drains quickly and remains warm while not drying out easily during warm weather. Many different kinds of vegetables thrive in loamy soil, so try to introduce crop rotation so that you can quickly replenish nutrients in the soil.

Planting

Not all plants do well going directly into the ground. Some need to be started indoors in smaller containers. For those plants that will go straight into the ground, ensure you have the proper levels of fertilizer incorporated into the soil while you are plowing. If the temperature is cooler where you live, it's best to start your plants indoors and wait for the frost to pass before taking them outside for replanting into the ground (Urban Abroad, 2023).

Mulch Well

Mulching allows your plants to retain as much water as they can for as long as they can by reducing the evaporation rate. This means you will water your plants less frequently. Mulch also keeps the soil cool during the summer, which is beneficial to the roots of your plants—the more mulch, the better for your crops.

Weeding and Watering

Keeping your crops free of weeds allows the soil to get aeration and sunlight. The instructions at the back of the seed packet dictate how to water your plants. If the climate is drier, you may have to water your crops more often, especially if the temperature gets very hot. Drip systems are more efficient, providing water directly while limiting evaporation.

Harvest Time

At some point, you will have to harvest your crops. You must carefully select the ripe fruit or vegetables, but it can be easy to become impatient. Watching your harvest come to life before your eyes can be exciting, but allow your produce enough time to ripen.

Basic Tools

Having the right tools can make backyard gardening something pleasurable to do. You need to have high-quality tools so that you can work well. Avoid plastic tools, and shop for bargains in local hardware stores and nurseries. Find and maintain the following tools:

1. garden hoe

2. garden shovel or D-handle shovel

3. leaf rake

4. scuffle hoe

5. dirt rake

6. hand tools (gardening gloves, pruner, trowel, transplanter, hoe, cultivator, weeder, garden seeder).

In addition to tools, there are a few other supplies you will find useful:

1. jute twine

2. twist ties (I use the ones I save from cord ties when I have to buy electronics)

3. 10oz spray bottle (I use recycled ones that are thoroughly cleaned)

4. plant labels

5. garden stakes (For seedlings, I use leftover chop-sticks)

Treat your garden tools like you would a good knife. Maintain their sharpness and keep them clean so that you can protect their longevity. Regular cleaning can also help prevent disease.

Year-Round Growth

Some plants grow all year round, while others are seasonal. If you plan accordingly, you may produce all year long by staggering different types of crops. Below is an example of what you can plant and when you can plant it.

- Warm weather crops: beans, potatoes, pumpkin, and eggplant do well in the spring, while tomatoes, cucumbers, peppers, and leafy greens thrive in the summer.

- Cool weather crops: fall crops include kale, cabbage, beets, and garlic, and those that can withstand winter cold are Brussels sprouts, collards, leeks, and carrots.

Planting Location

You have so many options on how to begin your backyard garden. You can grow your vegetables in containers, especially if you have limited space or want to do indoor gardening. Always ensure that the roots of potted plants are protected during winter, as the roots do not have the same insulation as plants growing from the ground. It's a good idea to start small and work your way up. Go for variety instead of raising a large amount of one thing. Diversity creates a healthier ecosystem and reduces pest outbreaks (Pesaturo, 2014).

Another option is having raised beds, making soil amending and weeding easier. Ensure your raised beds are narrow enough to reach the middle for weeding and harvesting. Vertical gardening is a new trend taking over backyard gardening (Pesaturo, 2014). Vertical gardening can maximize your produce if you have a small space, as you grow upward and not outward.

Using flower pots is also a good idea if you live in an urban area, and they come in all shapes and sizes. Use the proper potting soil for your plants to ensure they produce their best crop. Vining vegetables do well in hanging pots; this is like an upside-down version of vertical planting, as the plant has ample space to grow and produce vegetables. Planters are usually rectangular in shape, and herbs and small flowers tend to thrive in window box planters. Shrub-like plants do well in planters. There are many kinds of containers that will work. I have used horse troughs and barrels I collected at the salvage yard. With a drill to make drainage holes and some paint, you can make your garden not only productive but an interesting and pretty space that expresses your personality.

Community gardens are a great option if you don't have much space.

Grow Veggies Indoors

You may not have a backyard or acres of land to take advantage of to start your backyard gardening journey. You can still adopt a sustainable habit of growing your own food. It is possible to grow your own vegetables indoors as long as you have a spot in your home that receives up to six hours of sunlight a day, or you can use grow lights to guarantee the adequate growth of your plants (Martin, 2020).

You can choose high-quality potting soil or even go hydroponic, where your indoor garden has no soil at all. The best vegetables for indoor growing include arugula, herbs, beets, mushrooms, radishes, peppers, kale, chives, baby spinach, and lettuce. You have to choose the right containers for your plants that also fit into the area you have dedicated for them in your home. The containers should have drainage holes and can be anything from wooden planters to fabric pots. The right potting soil has a healthy mix of vermiculite, perlite, and coco peat. You want to create a warm and moist environment for the roots of your plants to grow in. Some soil is enhanced with fertilizer and worm castings to improve its nutrient content.

Vegetables need at least six hours of sunlight each day to grow adequately. Light is like a growth elixir for plants: The more they get, the more they grow. A south-facing window that receives uninterrupted sunlight is a perfect place to put your plants in front of.

If you are a fan of mushrooms, they do not require any sunlight, and you can put a mushroom kit just about anywhere in your home. There are several varieties of mushroom kits you can buy, including button, oyster, and reishi mushrooms. It can take less than 20 days for mushrooms to be ready to harvest, so you can enjoy your investment right away (Martin, 2020).

Keep your home at a constant temperature. Most plants will thrive if the temperature stays between 65°F and 75°F. If the air gets too dry or the plant is placed too close to a heat source, the plant suffers and dries out very quickly. A humidifier can help to introduce much-needed moisture to the air (Ly, 2021).

You should also remember to keep your watering consistent, so the fruit of your labor grows at the same rate, and open the windows for some fresh air occasionally to maintain good air quality for your vegetables.

By simply ensuring that these different components provide an ideal environment for your plants, you can have a budding indoor vegetable patch that any small farmer would envy.

A Pest Problem

Although you can make progress trying to become healthier and save money by growing your own food, some things can derail that process relatively quickly, and pests are one of them. When I first started backyard gardening, I was frustrated by how in a matter of days, my healthy plants could suddenly become limp and discolored due to creatures I didn't even know I had in my yard. I began to notice, in horror, that nothing was safe. It put me in a dilemma because toxic pesticides were not an option for me, so how would I stop these minuscule menaces from destroying the realization of my green thumb dreams? The first step I took was identifying the pests to learn more about them. The following are common garden pests (Miller, 2023):

- Aphids cut into plant tissue to suck away at the sap. You'll notice your plants' stunted growth or puckered leaves when aphids take over. They also attract ants from a sweet substance they secrete. The ants protect the aphids from other insect predators, so they must be controlled too.

- Cutworms are moth larvae that feed on plants during the night. They eat through stems, the part of the plant they come across first.

- Japanese beetles eat leaves until only their framework is left.

- Scales appear as bumps on plants and suck on their sap, turning leaves yellow and causing them to die.

- Slugs pop up when it gets rainy or in humid conditions. They feed at night.

- Spider Mites are arachnids that feed on plant juices and will turn the leaves yellow to gray until they drop off.

- Squash bugs inject a toxin into the plant and suck the sap right out of it with their sharp, sucking mouthparts. This causes yellow spots that eventually turn brown.

- Whiteflies are tiny sucking insects that stunt plant growth and leave behind a honeydew that leads to fungal disease.

Luckily, some tried and tested organic pest control methods have proven to work over the years.

Use the tips in this section to tackle pests in your garden in an organic and eco-friendly way.

1. Use 10–15 drops of peppermint, chrysanthemum, pine, or tea tree essential oil in one cup of water to effectively deter pests.

2. Practice crop rotation to kill off any bugs waiting for the next sowing season.

3. Insect traps can lessen the number of bugs in your garden. Place yellow cards that have a sticky substance on them around your garden to catch many unwanted pests. Small dishes filled with beer will attract earwigs, snails, and slugs (Miller, 2023).

4. Plant pungent-smelling herbs near other crops, like chives, or plants that grow year-round, like coriander or garlic, to deter pests (Amy, 2017). Nasturtiums are not pungent but also deter pests while being edible and beautiful (Johnson, 2023).

5. Make an effective organic pesticide (Savanah, 2016) with one tablespoon of crushed garlic, one tablespoon of cayenne pepper, half a gallon of distilled water, one tablespoon of unscented Castile liquid soap, and 10–15 drops of peppermint essential oil. Mix the water, garlic, and cayenne pepper, and leave to soak overnight. Strain the mixture with a cheesecloth and pour it into a spray bottle. Add the peppermint oil and Castile soap; shake vigorously to combine. Spray at the base of your vegetable plant and on leaves that are under attack. Avoid spraying fruit or vegetables directly, or they may end up tasting like peppermint.

6. Diatomaceous earth (DE) is a form of silica from fossilized aquatic microorganisms. Although it is non-toxic, take care not to get it on the skin or inhale it because it is an irritant. You can dilute DE with water and spray it on plants. I will become effective when it dries. DE is not suitable for places with a lot of rain as it must be reapplied.

7. Neem oil is a great natural pest control for organic gardening. Mix four teaspoons of neem oil, two teaspoons of liquid soap, and a gallon of water. Shake and spray. Neem oil also can be purchased in concentrated form.

8. Pepper Spray can be made at home to repel caterpillars, spider mites, mayflies, and bugs—puree five hot peppers in two cups of water. Add a teaspoon of liquid soap and strain before spaying (Campbell, 2019).

9. You can promote beneficial insects to your garden to help control pest species. These beneficial creatures include ladybugs, praying mantis, dragonflies, braconid wasps, and minute pirate bugs (Campbell 2019). Some of these insects can be purchased to be added to your garden, while others you simply need to recognize so you can avoid killing them if possible.

10. Thin out seedlings. Small weak plants are more likely to become diseased, and crowding will prevent air circulation. Prune away dead shoots and clear away leaf litter from around the base of your plants that can harbor pests and their eggs.

11. Companion planting can help deter insect pests for particular groups of vegetables. Growing carrots and onions together can keep carrot flies and onion maggots under control (Siegal, 2020).

12. Install bird and bat houses. Providing a home for insect predators will help limit insect pests and provide entertainment when you are relaxing in your beautiful garden.

Beneficial insects like ladybugs can help you control pests like aphids.

Create a Safe-Haven for Pollinators

Over 75% of all flowering plants are pollinated by insects or other animals (Planting for pollinators, 2017). Some fruits, like cucumbers, strawberries, and apples, grow from pollinated flowers. Other crops, like lettuce and broccoli, need pollination to produce seeds. This is not a process that happens spontaneously. Pollination is carried out by honey bees and bumblebees, flies, moths, beetles, and even bats.

You should include flowers and plants that attract pollinators to ensure your vegetables get all the help they need. Position your pollinator garden where it can receive at least six hours of sunlight (Dickenson, 2022). Find out what is native to your area and plant those flowers before others. If weeds flower, take your time to remove them, as they'll attract pollinators regardless. Leaving sugar water around your garden can feed exhausted pollinators and revive their purpose to pollinate everything. Make your garden pollinator-friendly, and the advantages for your vegetables and other crops will be endless.

Become an Urban Beekeeper

You don't need to live in the countryside to be a beekeeper. Having bees in an urban area is challenging, but it is not impossible. You can keep bees almost anywhere, as long as there is water close to the hive and a fence or shrubs to make sure the bees fly above your neighbor's home. A common location for beehives in the city is on a rooftop (The Growth and Feasibility of Urban Beekeeping, 2023). Make sure that keeping bees is allowed in your area to avoid penalties by your local authority. There will be a cost of buying or building a beehive and the following items:

- hive tool for $12
- beekeepers' jacket for $40

- smoker $40

- goatskin gloves $15

There are two types of hives: Langstroth hives, which stack boxes one upon the other as the hive grows, and top bar hives, which utilize horizontal beekeeping as additional frames are added to the back of the growing hive (Beauchamp, 2018).

For your neighbors, one of the scariest aspects of beehives is swarming, so be diligent in watching to avoid swarms. Some steps can be taken to reduce the chances of a swarm happening. Despite being scary, swarming bees are usually composed of bees with full stomachs and are docile and quiet (The Growth and Feasibility of Urban Bee-keeping, 2023).

If making your own hive is too challenging, you can buy or rent hives online. Source your bees from a reputable and approved dealer. Do not buy used supplies because there are a number of diseases hurting bee populations worldwide, and you don't want to contribute to their spread. Hand-holding and mentoring can help you avoid common mistakes, so it's a good idea to join a beekeeper's group. Never neglect your bees, and make arrangements for someone to tend to them should you be away for an extended period of time.

Solitary Bees

Although they won't provide you with honey, the small fly-like bees you see in the spring are great for pollination, and you can also give them a home. Although they have the ability to sting, they rarely do unless they are caught in your hand. They are important pollinators, and making a bee block to provide them with nesting habitat is easy.

For a bee block, a chunk of wood 4 inches wide, 6 inches deep, and a foot tall is a good size. You can use a left-over piece of log too. Drill holes of varying diameter (3/32" – 1/4") and depth (1-6 in.) close together on one face of the block. You can mix them up but put several of the same sizes next to each other in each row or column because similar species like to nest near each other. Put a small board on top to act as a roof to keep the rain out and secure it at least 3 feet above the ground. As the bees begin using the box, you will see them lining it with a papery substance of chewed vegetation. After laying her eggs, the hole will be closed up until the larvae emerge the following year.

Solitary bees are essential pollinators.

Store Your Harvest

Once your garden is up and running, you might find yourself with more produce than you can consume. Food preservation allows you to enjoy the fruits of your labor even when your crop is out of season. The following outlines the various easy ways you can preserve food:

1. Learn the basics of canning and know when to use pressure or water bath canning.

2. Store fruits and vegetables in vacuum-sealed bags in a chest freezer. Some veggies must be blanched first, then quickly dunked in cold water to lock in the flavor.

3. Dehydrated foods can last for long periods when vacuum-sealed. A dehydrator, an oven, and the sun can effectively preserve food.

4. Preserve your vegetables in vinegar by pickling them.

5. Roasting vegetables and storing them in oil can delay spoilage and mold formation.

6. Fermenting foods will keep them for much longer than pickling them. Lacto-fermenting (used to make traditional sauerkraut) is an easy way to ferment produce for preservation.

7. Airtight containers keep fruits and vegetables fresh for extended periods.

Canning Basics

Canning became extremely popular after John Mason invented the reusable "Mason Jar" in 1858 (Greenbaum and Rubinstein, 2012). There are many benefits to canning (Ewald 2014):

- Saves money because purchasing food in season can be cheaper.

- Preserves your harvest so you can enjoy it year-round.

- Prepares you for tough economic times.

- Eco-friendly because it prevents wasted food, limits packaging, and eliminates the need for food to be processed and shipped.

- Canned food from home will taste better, and you can adjust the taste with your own recipes.

- Canning provides healthier food that does not have additives and preservatives.

- You can turn your canned preserves into great personal gifts.

If you start canning, learning how to do it safely is essential. Done properly, the heat and pressure during canning destroy hazardous microorganisms and inactivates enzymes that cause food spoilage. The vacuum seal prevents microorganisms from getting back into the food. Several types of canning methods exist, including the water bath, steam canning, and pressure canning methods. Only the pressure canning method is safe for foods with low acidity (pH of more than 4.6). Avoid using the water bath or steam method with low-acid vegetables or meat (Johnson, 2021).

The water bath canning method does not require specialized equipment like steam or pressure canning. The jars are boiled underwater, which is safe for high-acid foods; for foods close to a pH of 4.6, lemon juice or citric acid can be added to make it safe. Steam canning is also for high-acid foods but uses less water, and the critical temperature needed is reached faster, so this method uses less energy (McKay, 2020). Only pressure canning allows for a high enough temperature for foods with low acidity to make the preserves safe. For beginners, I recommend the water bath method. It is not complicated, and it is easy to find recipes online. Make sure to do your research and follow the instructions. Several variables affect how you pack the preserves; for example, raw versus cooked vegetables or canning at high elevations may require different methods.

You can enjoy your harvest year-round by using canning or any of the other simple methods of preserving food listed above. It is a good feeling to look at shelves of organic produce that you have preserved yourself, knowing exactly what is in each jar and knowing you are prepared to care for yourself and your family under any eventuality.

From backyard produce to building your own hive, sustainability is all about doing what you can. This chapter is a resource for making money and growing your own food. The next chapter will focus on eating in a way that won't harm your pocketbook or the environment. With all this information, I know you're buzzing to get started, so go on, take flight!

6

A Healthy Diet– the Organic Way

Climate scientists and experts agree that the best diet includes few animal products. They believe a sustainable diet consists of a lot of fruit, plant-based proteins, and vegetables. Unfortunately, processed foods have become a part of our daily lives. The American Heart Association recommends that people eat minimally processed foods combined with the fresh food mentioned above to maintain a heart-healthy diet (Ettinger, 2021).

Research shows a sustainable diet can save money (Ettinger, 2021). A flexitarian, vegetarian, or vegan diet can drastically cut grocery expenses by up to one-third (Ettinger, 2021). The food we eat plays a significant role in whether or not we maintain a sustainable lifestyle. You may also want to increase your chances of living a long life to reap the benefits of the eco-friendly habits you are starting today. This chapter explores what eating organic entails and how it can positively contribute to a healthy body, a sustainable environment, and savings on your daily food expenses.

The Future Is Organic

The word "organic," when referring to food, means that the food is a product of organic farming. This means that anything that comes in contact with the produce be it a pesticide or fertilizer, must be made of a mixture of organic compounds.

Non-organic food, also called "conventional" food, may contain synthetic chemicals (from pesticides and fertilizers) that ensure the food is pest and weather-resistant to guarantee an adequate supply for the community. Conventional food can be unhealthy because it may have genetically modified components that negatively affect your health (Houston, 2022). Moreover, non-organic meat and poultry can have hormones and antibiotics in them that also interfere with the normal functioning of your body. Whenever possible, it makes more sense for the long term, for your body and the environment, to choose organic food.

The agriculture industry continues to farm in such a way that it consistently releases an alarming amount of greenhouse gasses into the environment. Organic farming releases a smaller amount of greenhouse gas emissions. Growing food organically can revive biodiversity and introduce a variety of life in and around your produce. For example, earthworms enjoy rich, wet soil that contains a lot of organic matter, such as on an organic farm, and they secrete concentrated levels of organic and mineral compounds; once they die, they decompose quickly to add to the health of the soil.

Non-renewable, oil-based fertilizers and pesticides may not always be available for use (Wales, 2019). Farming organic food relies on eco-friendly pesticides and fertilizers derived from animals or plants. In this way, the soil remains safe to use, the produce is healthy to eat, and the workers on the farm do not come into contact with harmful substances.

Organic farming makes the soil healthier by preventing toxic pesticides and fertilizers from seeping into groundwater supplies (Wales, 2019). The state of the water and soil on the farm will determine the quality of the food produced.

Further, organic food tastes much better than processed food, giving you more pronounced, natural, fresh flavors that make eating a much more pleasurable experience. Embrace organic food and see how many non-organic foods you can eliminate from your diet.

Why Organic Food?

The benefits of switching to an organic diet are numerous. Hopefully, these advantages inspire you to make a few changes and start experimenting with organic food. Non-organic food is usually packed with sodium or sugar and rarely tastes fresh. Organic food tastes better and is more nutrient-dense (Brooke, 2020). Most processed foods are fortified with minerals and vitamins, whereas organic food naturally contains more vitamins, minerals, and other nutrients essential to good health.

Organic food will taste superior to your taste buds because your body can recognize that it is the best option for your health. Genetically modified food may not be healthy for human consumption as its effects on long-term health are still unknown. Food that is not genetically modified, like organic produce, is the best way to ensure a healthy diet.

Organic fruits and vegetables are rich in antioxidants that can help prevent disease and cognitive dysfunction, and eating organic foods can reduce exposure to toxic heavy metals (10 reasons why organic food is better for your clients, 2019).

Eating seasonal food grown locally that doesn't spend time being transported can ensure you eat more nutrient-dense produce. If fresh produce leaves an organic farm today and is on your dinner table tomorrow, it will retain more nutrients and be exposed to fewer bacteria and diseases. You can taste the difference, and your body will gain more nutrients and minerals; local organic farmers will also be empowered by community support.

There is less travel (that uses fuel) and less packaging (that may contain harmful plastics) when you choose local organic farms to source food, which will ultimately reduce pollution. When you buy produce from big supermarket chains, you are feeding into a system that harms the environment because that produce arrives on a truck, train, or plane powered by fossil fuel and may be packaged in various types of plastic that are not sustainable to the environment. No matter which angle you look at it from, organic food is better for the economy, the environment, and your health.

Get Invested in an Eco-Friendly Diet

Because you are reading this book, you are likely interested in reducing your carbon footprint and living a more sustainable lifestyle. To contribute to this goal, you can consider eating a sustainable diet. You might think eating organically is the only aspect of maintaining a sustainable diet, but the concept has numerous layers. An eco-friendly diet requires you to make several changes to your diet in addition to eating organically.

A sustainable diet is one that can support human health and that can support natural systems without contributing to their degradation and pollution. Eating a sustainable diet will ensure that your health is bolstered in the long term and that the environment is preserved for generations to come. Going organic will reduce the number of harmful pesticides and fertilizers used to grow food, meaning the working conditions for farm workers are also improved. There are various ways to maintain a sustainable diet, which are discussed below.

A Plant-Based Diet

Having a diet primarily focused on fresh produce does not mean you cannot eat meat or dairy products. You may enjoy better health if you eat mainly plant-based foods like nuts, legumes, fruits, vegetables, and plant-based proteins. The average American consumes 45% more meat per week than the US Department of Agriculture recommends. This, combined with lower exercise, has led to an increase in obesity and some forms of cancer (Ebadi, Willett, and Stordalen, 2015)

A plant-based diet also contributes to better environmental health. Close to 40% of the land in the world is used for agricultural purposes (both farming and livestock rearing), which is why over a third of all greenhouse gas emissions are derived from farming and animal production (Byrne, 2022). To effectively reduce greenhouse gas emissions from agricultural land use, it is beneficial to the climate to eat less meat and more plants because livestock releases methane and nitrous oxide into the atmosphere.

Minimize Waste

Buying only what you need to eat and using all the ingredients in your pantry and fridge can reduce food waste. If a community consumes a lot of food, the grocery chains and supermarkets feel pressured to bring in more and more food to meet demand. The transportation of all this food increases the carbon footprint. Unfortunately, in the end, much of this food is not consumed but is thrown away. The Environmental Protection Agency estimates that each year, U.S. food loss and waste embody 170 million metric tons of carbon dioxide equivalent. This equals the annual CO_2 emissions of 42 coal-fired power plants (Buzby, 2022)

Finding ways to reduce the amount of food waste in your home can contribute to its sustainability. Fresh produce can spoil very quickly, so try to cook and consume it as soon as possible. Find ways to utilize scraps and freeze any leftovers to be consumed later. Many of us have enjoyed left-over turkey in soups, casseroles, and sandwiches. You also do not have to throw away plant scraps as they can be used to create a compost heap. If you have too much of one thing (like too many lemons from your lemon tree or a mountain of strawberries bought during a sale), you can share it with your neighbors and loved ones.

Buy Only Sustainable Food

If your goal is to eat a sustainable diet, you should be sure that the food you eat is produced sustainably. There are food producers that only use regenerative agriculture to grow their food, and these are the producers that you should align yourself with, as they use methods of farming that benefit the soil they farm on (Loewe, 2023b). How they grow their food keeps the soil healthy, which helps keep the ecosystem on the farm in equilibrium. Sustainable food producers avoid toxic pesticides and fertilizers, which can compromise the soil and groundwater. Additionally, these farmers use sustainable farming methods such as crop rotation so that the land can rest between harvests and regain its nutrients.

Look for the United States Department of Agriculture (USDA) organic label on foods, which requires farmers to meet criteria that maintains sustainability. However, this label is not always a guarantee that the products are sustainable. Feel free to ask producers questions about their farming practices, especially at local farmer's markets where this label may not be available to smaller-scale farmers.

Mindful Eating

Practicing eating mindfully can help you to maintain a more sustainable diet. Eating mindfully requires you to be present in the moment and to use all your senses to enjoy the food experience. Try being fully engaged when creating a meal, from what you buy and where you buy it to how the food is prepared to the dining experience. This will create opportunities for you to think about how the food was produced and whether or not it is organic or genetically modified. You will also appreciate the look and feel of different foods, the taste, the colors, and the diverse textures.

Eating slowly and taking time to chew your food for longer allows your brain time to receive the signal when the stomach is full, thus reducing overeating. When you eat quickly, it is easy to overeat. You may find that you don't need as much food as you previously thought. Overconsumption is reduced when you eat mindfully, and mindful eating improves your food choices. Mindful eating also will help you to maintain a sustainable diet for longer.

A Sustainable Eating Plan

Okay, now it's time to spring into action! This section will guide you on food choices to create a more sustainable eating plan. You may be scratching your head about what you need to do to get started; this part of the book will outline what you should eat more of and what you should avoid.

You already know to avoid meat products and rely more on plants because they place less stress on the environment and take fewer resources to grow. The following foods have a low environmental footprint (lower greenhouse gas emissions) and require less land and water to grow. This is just a starting point, and you can expand this list for yourself after research.

1. Organic produce, like potatoes, onions, carrots, celery, and seasonal fruits, that are locally sourced can ensure the soil is kept healthy and does not pose a threat to your health. Check whether or not the food is grown in climate-controlled greenhouses, which can contribute to greenhouse gas emissions.

Food grown outdoors is often better for the environment, as fewer resources are needed to tend to it. Certain crops attract pests and are more likely to be heavily dosed with harmful pesticides, such as strawberries, kale, spinach, mustard, and collard greens. If you are unsure where they come from, it is best to avoid these foods, as these pesticides cannot be removed by simply washing them (Loewe, 2023a).

2. Certain nuts, such as peanuts (not really a nut but treated as one, so included), macadamia nuts, hazelnuts, and Brazil nuts, are great for a sustainable diet. However, other nuts, like cashews and almonds, are unsustainable (Caps, Bots, and Scherer, 2022). Choosing a nut variety that does not harm the environment can be tricky because some nuts grown in other countries use less water, but the processing and shipping increase the CO_2 footprint. However, when it comes to adding protein to your diet, all nuts are more eco-friendly per gram of protein than livestock.

3. Growing grains like barley, oats, and rye produce lower greenhouse gas emissions than grain like rice. Most communities around the world rely on grains as their diet staple because they are cheap to grow. Unfortunately, this also means the demand for grains is relatively high. Due to this, grains are cultivated in monocultures, pieces of land used to grow only one crop type. This type of farming is harmful to the soil, depleting most of its nutrients. Therefore, always consider where you purchase your grains from and aim to buy from small-scale farmers who utilize eco-friendly farming techniques.

4. The production of legumes like lentils, chickpeas, and beans results in minimal greenhouse gas emissions. Growing these crops benefits farm ecosystems as legumes release nitrogen into

the ground, restoring the soil's health and nutrients. Legumes also serve as a source of plant-based protein so that you can rely less on red meat as a source of protein.

5. Seaweed is gaining popularity as a crop to grow for consumption. This crop benefits the environment because it filters out pollutants in the water and spreads quickly, with little human intervention. The ease of growing seaweed has made it an attractive crop for U.S. farmers on the coast. This also means its availability is growing, making it easy to find in local grocery stores.

Less sustainable food options include the following:

- Lamb, as sheep, emit methane and need vast areas of land to maintain and feed.

- Beef, because cattle emit high levels of methane.

- Goats are also ruminants, and their rearing is linked to high greenhouse gas emissions.

- Milk and dairy products like cheese, yogurt, and butter because they are by-products of cattle.

- Carbonated soft drinks due to the harmful plastic packaging they come in and their transportation requirements.

Using your protein as the star of your dish can also be considered an unsustainable food choice. You can prepare protein as an accompaniment for your vegetables rather than as the focal point. Take the time to make your vegetables and plant proteins more attractive so that you are more enthused to consume them. Integrating sustainable foods into your diet will lower your home's carbon footprint, making your home more eco-friendly. You might even notice some savings on your grocery bill.

The Danger of Microplastics

Plastic is everywhere, and you may be eating it, too. Microplastics are tiny microscopic particles you find in the environment due to numerous years of disposal and disintegration of consumer products (Batista, 2022). When plastic was first created, it was considered innovative and revolutionary. The world soon began to make many things out of this new, robust, durable material. There were even houses that were made out of plastic.

Eventually, after extensive research, plastic was found to be a harmful material to the environment, as it does not break down easily in nature. The breakdown of plastic occurs over a very long period, and because it is not biodegradable, it breaks down into small pieces, permeating the atmosphere, soil, food, and water. Microplastics have been found to be harmful to human health because they can negatively affect your reproductive, developmental, and hormonal health. It can increase your risk of developing chronic diseases and compromise your immune system.

Microplastics are found mainly in fruits and vegetables, salt, bottled water, tea bags, rice, fish and shellfish, beer, and honey (Batista, 2022). To avoid eating microplastics, it is better to choose tap water and eco-friendly water bottles. There are manufacturers of plastic-free kitchen utensils, pots, crockery, and cutlery. Purchasing items made from materials like bamboo can reduce the amount of microplastics in the food we eat.

Because you may be used to using plastic containers, it is generally not easy to switch to a plastic-free life, but you can start small and grow from there. You can replace children's plastic toys with wooden ones. Look around to see if your area has zero-waste stores containing plastic-free products. Avoid processed foods, as they can contain high levels of microplastics, and select glass or stainless steel over plastic bottles. Although the levels of microplastics in tap water are lower than in bottled water, you may still have to filter the tap water to lower the levels further.

When you store leftovers in plastic containers, you might, later on, warm them up in the same containers. When heat is applied, solid plastic creates microplastic much more quickly, and heating food in plastic containers transfers microplastic to your food (Batista, 2022). Avoid microwaving leftovers, or any food, in plastic containers.

Cups that contain high-density polyethylene (HDPE)-grade plastic are considered safe. Yet, studies show they tend to leak estrogenic chemicals into the liquid put into them (Batista, 2022). Cleaning products can also contain microplastics, so try to source plastic-free cleaning supplies that limit the microplastics that find their way into your food. Due to the amount of plastic dumped into oceans and lakes over the years, some aquatic life may contain high levels of microplastics. You may want to reduce the amount of seafood you consume, as microplastics have been found in their muscle tissue, which is often the part that humans consume.

If you want to step it up a notch, you can reduce the amount of plastic in your home by purchasing plastic-free cosmetics, decorations, clothes, and packaging. By lowering your interaction and contact with plastic, you can reduce the microplastics you and your family consume.

How to Enjoy a Nutritious Vegetarian Diet

Knowing how to get the most nutrition out of a vegetarian diet will not only help the environment, but it can also improve your health and minimize your risk of developing heart disease, diabetes, and some cancers (Mayo Clinic Staff, 2020). Heart healthy diets also appear to reduce the chance of developing Alzheimer's disease.

A concern with the vegetarian diet is that it can lead to an over-reliance on processed food, which often contains fat, sugar, sodium, and many empty calories. Another concern with a vegetarian diet is protein: Most people get their daily intake of protein from red meat, poultry, or fish. However, with a bit of planning, you can create a vegetarian diet that meets the needs of your entire family.

Firstly, you should be able to differentiate between the various types of diets before choosing which one is a good fit for you. The main differences are based on what you are allowed to eat along with your plant-based diet.

- A vegan diet does not allow meat, fish, poultry, eggs, dairy, or any other food derived from animal products.

- A pescatarian diet allows one to eat only fish, seafood, eggs, dairy, fruits, and vegetables, excluding poultry and meat.

- A lacto-ovo vegetarian diet does not allow fish, meat, or poultry but allows the consumption of eggs and dairy products.

- An ovo-vegetarian diet forbids the consumption of seafood, dairy, poultry, and meat, but you may eat eggs.

- A lacto-vegetarian diet allows you to consume milk, yogurt, cheese, and butter, but not meat, fish, eggs, and poultry.

- A flexitarian diet is one which is primarily vegetarian but also includes dairy, eggs, meat, fish, and poultry every other day or in limited quantities.

Whatever diet you choose, you should know how much of which food group to eat to meet recommended daily allowances. Following specific dietary guidelines for vegetarians, you can ensure you do not become nutrient deficient (Mayo Clinic Staff, 2020).

If you eat a 2,000-calorie diet daily, for example, you should eat:

- 2 cups of fruits
- 2 ½ cups of vegetables
- 3 cups of dairy (or vegan alternative)
- 6 ½ ounces of whole grains

- 3 ½ ounces of protein

- 27 grams of oils

These foods should be nutrient-dense, low-fat, and prepared in a healthy manner, such as steaming, grilling, or air-frying. Further, your food should not be prepared with additional salt, fats, sugar, or refined starch. Try not to be too strict with yourself when starting a plant-based diet, as it will be challenging to adhere to. Be cognizant of the foods you are eliminating, as you may rid your diet of necessary nutrients like vitamin B12, calcium, or vitamin D. Invest in some vegetarian cookbooks or search for vegetarian recipes online to still meet your body's nutritional needs. Find plant-based substitutes for meat that are not overly processed. Increase the number of meatless meals you have during the week, and add plant-based proteins to those meals to make them balanced.

Using food to reach your sustainability goals is an effective way to reduce your carbon footprint. Eating organic food and switching to a plant-based diet will likely improve your health, save money, and be more eco-friendly. Sustainability is an all-encompassing topic, and a large part of it is assessing your eating habits and adjusting them accordingly.

Similarly, the water you use and how you use it can affect the environment. Water is a precious resource that we need to conserve, as it is essential to the survival of many ecosystems and human life. Read on if you want to be like water and stay current.

7

Be Water Wise

Water is a precious resource, and we use it for almost everything in the home. Humans cannot survive without water. We use water to clean, bathe, cook, and grow plants. It is a life-giving substance that we will always need to thrive. We need to conserve water because we depend heavily on water to live a good life. The average American utilizes between 140–170 gallons of water daily. Water is used in various ways, but the most extensive domestic use is bathing and showering, which accounts for almost a third of water use in the home. A leaky faucet is one of the most detrimental ways water is wasted. Did you know that if every household in the United States of America had a leaky faucet that was dripping at least one drop per second, 928 million gallons of water would be wasted (Water Conservation Facts, 2019)?

An eco-friendly household does not waste water. You may not notice the water wastage in your home or wonder why your water bill is so high. If you feel genuinely concerned about how much water you use and how you can conserve water in your home, this chapter is tailored for you. I will go through various ways that water wastage can occur when you are home before delving into how you can conserve water. I was amazed at the small ways I could harvest water for use around my home and how much I was unknowingly wasting. In the end, you will be much more informed about how to avoid water waste in your home and benefit from a lower water bill. If you find yourself guilty of the many ways water is wasted in the home, don't feel bad about it because you are turning a new leaf and will soon know how to use water more wisely.

Why Your Water Meter Is Running Fast

Before we get to how to conserve water, you should understand where the waste occurs. We need fresh water to survive, and although most of the earth's surface is submerged in water, only about 1% of fresh water is on the planet. This is the water used for drinking and home consumption. According to the U.S. Environmental Protection Agency, a majority of households in the United States use around 300 gallons per day (Top 10 Ways You're Wasting Water, 2014).

If you're used to certain habits, it may be challenging to break them, but I guarantee it is not impossible. The following represent the various ways water gets wasted in most households.

- If you observe any leaks from your faucets or pipes in and around your home, you should repair or replace them as soon as possible. But what of hidden leaks? You may have a broken line and not know it. You should carefully scrutinize your water bill. You may be able to decipher whether or not you have a hidden leak somewhere in your home if there's a sudden increase in what you pay for water.

- Many people enjoy a healthy lawn, and in some areas, it is a requirement set by your local homeowner's authority. During the summer, you may feel you have to water your lawn often so that it does not dry out. Be careful not to overwater your lawn and stick to doing so in the morning and evening to avoid the high evaporation rate present during the hotter hours of the day. Plant drought-tolerant grass varieties if you must have a lawn. You should only need to water your lawn twice a week, at the very most.

- There is nothing like a hot shower to refresh your mind and relax your body. Unfortunately, conventional shower heads allow the maximum flow of water to run through them, and spending a lot of time in the shower can mean gallons of water wasted. To prevent this waste of water, it is best to install a low-flow shower head that guarantees only around two gallons of water used per minute. Try also to limit the amount of time you spend in the shower. Time your showers not to be more than three to five minutes. A five-minute shower can use up to 20 gallons of water; that's a lot of water for just one shower (Water Conservation Facts, 2019).

- Don't take baths regularly. Taking a bath can be a wonderfully relaxing activity; however, the average bathtub holds about 40 to 50 gallons (Kelsey, 2021). A shower can get you as clean using half the amount of water. Make taking a bath a special activity, for those days when you really worked your muscles or mind and earned the indulgence. It will feel even better.

- The convenience of a washing machine can have you washing loads that are not full. Leaving your laundry load only half full wastes not only water but also electricity. Think about filling up your washer so the load is full and making each wash more cost-effective for your water and energy bill. You will save money on detergent, too (Mathews, 2015).

- Older water fixtures will probably waste more water and cost you even more money on your water bill. According to the U.S.

Environmental Protection Agency, installing eco-friendly fixtures could reduce water consumption by about 30 percent (5 Simple Ways to Stop Wasting Water Around the House, 2018). Nowadays, there are water-wise fixtures that your plumber can install to conserve water in your home. As mentioned above, an eco-friendly shower head can save you around three gallons of water per minute.

Water Conservation

Now that you know how water can be wasted, you can jump into action and attempt to reduce waste in your home. The simple methods mentioned in this section can save money on your water bill and conserve fresh water. Again, your creativity is key. The more you practice the suggestions in this section, the more creative you will become at conserving water in and around your home.

Reuse, Reuse, Reuse

Believe it or not, you do not have to use water only once before you pour it down the drain. The water you use to wash your fruits and vegetables you can keep to wash dishes or water your flower beds. When you turn on the tap, ensure you capture the water in a container or the sink so that it can be reused for other things later. After cooking rice or pasta, drain the water into a container and allow it to cool before using it to water your garden.

Switch to Handheld Showers

Showers use less water than baths, and with a handheld shower, you can direct the water flow to the specific body part you want to rinse off. It's almost impossible to hold the shower head and lather yourself up simultaneously, so you likely will do one thing at a time. Therefore, you will stop the water flow while still soaping your body up. Thus, a handheld shower will effectively reduce how much water you consume during a shower.

Strategize During Showers

Time yourself on how long you spend in the shower, then try to reduce that time minute by minute until you reach around five minutes. If you need to run the shower before the hot water hits the shower head, don't let the water run down the drain. You can get a bucket to catch the water that you will not use and find a way to use it in your garden; you can even use it to wash your shoes or to hand wash your delicates. When the shower water reaches the desired temperature, take that quick shower, making sure to keep it brief. Try to keep the shower's temperature luke-warm and not scalding hot so that less energy is used to heat the water.

Mend What You Can

Clothing takes a lot of water to make. An outfit consisting of a pair of jeans and a simple t-shirt can take up to 2,721 gallons to make (Daman, 2019). If you can repair or mend the clothes you already have, do so, or buy pre-loved clothes from second-hand stores. Purchasing new clothes often means contributing to thousands of gallons of water used to make them.

Low-Flow is the Way To Go

One of the ways water gets wasted is because of the flow pressure in the faucets. You can save up to 26,000 gallons of water by installing low-flow shower heads, toilets, and faucets (5 Simple Ways to Stop Wasting Water around the House, 2018). A low-flow water fixture does not compromise the water pressure but reduces the amount of water used. Low-flow technology has evolved over the years and may cost more, but you will soon see the return on investment in a short time via savings on your water bill.

Aerate Your Lawn

Sometimes soil can get compacted, thus reducing the amount of water and nutrients it can absorb. If the ground beneath your grass does not take in much water, you must water it more. Periodically aerate your lawn so rainwater can soak into the ground when it rains. For the soil to remain healthy, you need to expose it to sunlight and oxygen. For example, you can aerate your lawn using a spike aerator, a tool that creates small pockets of air in the ground that allow water and nutrients to penetrate compacted soil areas. Aerated lawns take in much more rainwater, which means you will water it less with your freshwater resources (Trees.com Staff, 2018).

Don't Use All the Dishes

The more dishes you use, the more water you need to wash them. Often, after making a delicious meal, you may want to serve it in a beautiful dish. Unnecessary transfers of the meal into extravagant dishes create more mess that will need more gallons of water to clean. You can serve food in the pot it was cooked in so that you use less water to clean up after dinner.

Cover the Pool and Hot Tub

Using a pool cover reduces evaporation and can reduce replacement water by 30-50% (Rinkesh, 2018). Of course, a pool cover also reduces heat loss and saves energy.

Water Harvesting

Using available freshwater can drive up your water bill. Fortunately, you have the choice of harvesting rainwater. This concept is not new, although it may be new to you.

Harvesting rainwater requires you to catch rainwater and not allow it to run off into the ground. Collecting it will cut down your water bill, as you will be relying on your stored rainwater as well as your fresh water supply. Additionally, the hard water that you may have to use to wash your clothes in your washing machine can do damage; rainwater is considered soft water. Therefore, limescale will not build up, and you will need even less detergent to wash your delicate clothes effectively.

If you live in a drought area, storing rainwater ensures that you always have an adequate water supply, even when the area is experiencing a drought. But do not use rainwater for drinking. Unbelievable as it sounds, scientists found that, after a decade-long investigation, when analyzed against US contamination guidelines, rainwater is unsafe for human consumption worldwide. This is due to PFAS levels, or per-and poly-fluoroalkyl substances (Thomas, 2022).

Using rainwater to water your garden makes it flourish more, as soft water is more nurturing to plants than hard water (6 financial and environmental reasons why rainwater harvesting should be encouraged, 2017). Having a water system in place and watching your reserves go down will make you more aware of the water you use in and around your home. Therefore, harvesting rainwater will make you more appreciative of the water that is available to you.

Rooftop Rainwater Harvesting

Rooftops are often the most common catchment for rainwater. Rooftop harvesting requires the roof to catch the rainwater as it falls. It is then transferred to a tank or a recharge system. Components involved in rooftop rainwater harvesting are affordable and contain various sub-components such as catchments, transportation, first flush, and filters (Raja, 2018).

a. Catchments are the areas that catch the water and add it to the system. This could be your sloping roof, your courtyard, or open ground.

b. This water must be transported using water pipes, gutters, or drain pipes. All lines should be U.V. resistant and have wire mesh in various places to filter out debris.

c. A device that flushes out the first shower of water so the system can begin to catch and store the rest of the rainwater is referred to as a first flush. It allows the first shower to wash away the leaves or silt that may have accumulated on the catchment.

d. Depending on what you wish to use it for, after passing through the first flush, water can be passed through a filter to remove microorganisms, bacteria, and color. Filters should be changed often to avoid clogging.

There are different uses of rooftop harvested water. Firstly, rainwater can be used directly from storage to the garden or be used to wash clothes. Secondly, rainwater can recharge groundwater aquifers, like boreholes, dug wells, trenches, ponds, and pits.

How to Harvest Rainwater

To begin collecting rainwater, you must guide your water in a specific direction. For example, if you are catching water that falls off of your roof, you need to install some gutters that will flow to a particular location. As the water flows toward its final destination, you need to have it run through a filter and have an overflow system located at the base of every catchment.

To collect the rainwater, have it flow into a rain barrel of your desired size. Using a rain chain instead of a downspout can add beauty and sound to the collection, and you can make them yourself. After that, you may further divert the rainwater to storage tanks to use it for various things. Having a water pump installed gives you the necessary pressure to wash cars and water trees in your garden with a garden hose.

Water is a precious resource, and you should strive to conserve it whenever possible. Whatever little ways you can come up with to reuse water or minimize the amount you use daily will count toward a lower water bill and reduce the burden on freshwater resources.

8

Conserve Energy

When you wake up in the morning, you already know what to do to prepare for your day. Perhaps you need to switch on the light, make some coffee, or watch the news. Your breakfast needs to be made, and your shower water should be lukewarm to hot. All these tasks require energy to power the appliances that will facilitate them. Your home needs the energy to run. Leading a sustainable life means having an energy-efficient home.

In early 2019, the U.S. surpassed 2 million solar system installations. This milestone comes just three years after the industry completed its one-millionth installation, a feat that took 40 years to accomplish. Most notably, the solar industry will reach 4 million installations in 2023. Solar is the fastest-growing energy resource in the world (Moxie, 2020). Increases in solar system installation indicate that more and more Americans are becoming energy conscious. Solar power is gaining popularity as a method of making the home more energy efficient. Of course, you can achieve an energy-efficient home in numerous ways, and this chapter is focused on teaching you about all of those options.

An Energy-Efficient Home

An energy-efficient home is one that is built airtight and well-insulated. This makes it easier for heating and cooling equipment to get the house to the right temperature without using excessive energy. An energy-efficient home has low utility bills and low water consumption. The various cost-saving methods that can be implemented to conserve energy in your home range from moderately priced to expensive. Choose the way that suits your budget and lifestyle; make a plan (and a budget) to work toward the rest.

Insulate Properly

When a home is built, it is usually insulated. This means that insulating material is placed within the walls and the roofing that helps disrupt the movement of heat energy. In the cold winter months, heat can remain within the home, and during the warm summer months, heat from outside is prevented from entering.

A well-insulated home allows you to have better control of heat energy. If your insulation is poor, it will be easy for the heat to escape from your home during the winter. You may compensate for this with more heating, but this will drastically increase your energy bill and harm the environment in the process. Research how you can insulate your home yourself, or find an expert to ensure your home is insulated properly.

Energy-Efficient Fixtures and Appliances

Appliance manufacturers have made significant changes in how their appliances use energy. These appliances are made so they don't use excessive power to run and have a smaller carbon footprint. Because eco-friendly appliances use less energy, this leads to fewer greenhouse gasses and helps to slow global warming. An energy-efficient home has appliances that need smaller amounts of water to function, too (afox, 2019).

The lightbulbs you use can also help inch you closer to a more sustainable home. Compact fluorescent lightbulbs (CFLs) consume less energy than traditional light bulbs, although their initial cost is more. CFLs last much longer (up to 10 times) than standard bulbs. Even if you don't change the bulbs in your home all at once, you will see a noticeable difference in your energy bill, even with just a few CFLs.

Appliances that conserve energy should still be used sparingly. Overuse can still increase energy use, increasing utility bills and CO_2 emissions. If your thermostat temperature is adjusted too many times or you rely too much on your space heater during winter, it can lead to overuse of the appliance. Your home's temperature should remain neutral, not too hot or too cool. If a device is not in use, switch it off and unplug it. Energy can be wasted if an appliance is plugged into a socket, even if it is switched off.

Solar Power

Solar power is taking the world by storm and for a good reason. Solar panels allow you to create energy that can be used within the home by converting sunlight into electricity. They are an excellent investment and contribute to making your home more energy-efficient.

Solar panels for your home can be pretty pricey, hence why they are considered an investment; once installed, they can almost eliminate your energy costs, depending on what they are installed to power. More on solar power will be discussed further in this chapter.

Smart Home Systems

Everyone enjoys having convenience in their home. Smart Home features are a good investment from a sustainability standpoint because they combine comfort, security, and efficiency. Usually, the system entails a central place where you can monitor and control various integrated functions, such as your appliances, lighting, security, utilities, and temperature. Sometimes, you can get your coffee maker running without being in the same room.

To create a smart home, you need a home hub that serves as the control center (Lamkin, 2023). This device will integrate all the other smart devices in your home and manage them from one central place. There are various brands you can choose as a home hub, but they'll give you the freedom to control dozens of devices, from lights to thermostats to security systems and window blinds. As the home hub is the starting point, spend time choosing one and ensure you get one that works for your home.

To monitor electricity usage in your household, utility companies install an electricity meter for billing purposes, which can help you keep an eye on power consumption. The meter measures use in the kilowatt hour (kWh) but is generally installed in hidden or inaccessible places. Smart energy meters give you access to your consumption rate over a wireless connection and can identify which appliances use the most power. From there, you can make an informed decision about what you will do to reduce your energy costs.

Smart lighting systems allow you to control the lights in your house remotely or automatically. Lights on a timer can be especially useful when you are away from home but want lights on in the evening to make it look like you are home. Remotely controlling the lights from a mobile device will allow you to turn lights off that you or the kids forgot to turn off after leaving a room or the house.

A comfortable home is one where the temperature and environment are soothing to the occupants. Smart thermostats put the power of comfort in your hands. Using that technology, you can control the heating and air conditioning and anticipate specific needs depending on the weather. For example, if it's a hot summer, you'll need to keep a consistently cool temperature. Sudden changes in temperature settings will burden your system and waste energy.

Security is another feature you can integrate into your Smart Home system. On top of being notified in real-time when there's an intruder, you can also automate when your alarm system is armed and unarmed. Other security features can be programmed into the system, like turning the lights on when there is an intruder or locking doors and windows.

Overall, the improvement in Smart Home technology can make the running of your home more energy efficient and, therefore, more sustainable.

Replace Your Windows

Windows allow heat to escape from your home during the winter and cool air to leak out during the summer. If your home is losing a lot of heat or cool air, you may have to use more energy to keep it warm or cool. Some older windows are less efficient than newer models. Consider installing a double-panel window and vinyl frame. Single-pane windows and aluminum frames are unfavorable for a sustainable home (Rinkesh, 2014). Tinting your windows can also prevent too much sunlight from entering the house and heating it up during summer. Some quick research can help you find local companies that can help you get better windows to make your home more sustainable. If you don't own the house you live in or don't have the budget to renovate, consider the window tint option first.

Renewable Energy Is the Best Way to Power Your Home

Most urban homes depend on electricity to run. The combustion of fossil fuels is most commonly what generates the electricity you use daily. This kind of power is not renewable and is harmful to the environment. You don't have to depend on this energy source to keep your home running, especially if it does more harm than good. If you harness the power of renewable energy, you can make your home much more eco-friendly while saving money on your electric bill. You have various options you can choose from to power your home so that you can stay away from electricity powered by natural gas, coal, and nuclear power. As sustainable technology evolves, eco-conscious engineers develop various ways to power your home using renewable energy. Now numerous options allow you to reduce your carbon footprint, save money, and keep your home running efficiently.

Solar Power

Solar power is a relatively affordable renewable energy source for homes and commercial buildings. It offers the cheapest electricity that runs on the sun's power. Purchasing solar panels and installing them will cost you, as you can expect to pay anything between $16,730 to $30,970. The cost will depend on how many solar panels you install and who is installing them. Due to the rising popularity of this type of renewable energy, you can almost be sure that the price of a solar panel system will soon become more affordable. Suppose you want to calculate how much you will save on electricity by installing a solar panel system. In that situation, you have to look at various factors, such as your rate of electricity consumption, where your roof is facing, the amount of sunlight available, and the size of your solar panel system (Price to Compare, n.d.).

To find out what a solar panel system will cost for your home, you need to consult a solar expert in your area to give you an estimate. Finding research done on homes located in a similar climate or region can also give you a picture of what you may have to invest in financially.

If you cannot install solar panels on the home you live in, you may still be able to benefit from this renewable energy source if there are community solar projects close to you. Community solar is a farm or garden project that utilizes solar panel systems shared by numerous people in the same locality. In this way, you can enjoy the benefits of a solar panel system without paying for the purchase or installation of the solar panels (Price to Compare, n.d.).

Finally, if you can't afford a solar system for your entire house, consider using portable solar panels for designated energy needs, such as your greenhouse or hot tub.

Geothermal Energy

Geothermal energy systems harness the power of heat already in the earth. This type of renewable energy can heat or cool your home by using a system of pipes that are buried deep beneath your home. Due to the depth of the lines, this system can take advantage of the heat or water found beneath the earth and use that to regulate the temperatures in your home. Depending on what you want, the geothermal system can either draw heat from the ground and warm your home or extract heat from it and release it back into the ground or a body of water to keep your home cool. According to the EPA, high-efficiency geothermal systems are, on average, 48 percent more efficient than gas furnaces, 75 percent more efficient than oil furnaces, and 43 percent more efficient when in the cooling mode (Price to Compare, n.d.).

What you can expect to spend on installing a geothermal system depends on your home's size, your locality, and the availability of geothermal contractors and experts in your area. A geothermal system typically costs twice as much as a conventional HVAC system (Price to Compare, n.d.). However, because this system is more efficient than air conditioning or furnace heating, you may see energy savings that guarantee a return on investment on installation costs within ten years or less. Additionally, make sure to look for a tax break. Federal and state tax credits traditionally have been available for installing a geothermal system, and they can add up to significant savings.

Hydroelectric Power

This kind of renewable energy is an option if you live near a body of water, such as the ocean, a lake, or a stream. If the body of water is permanent throughout the year and not seasonal, hydroelectric power becomes a reliable source of renewable energy. Hydropower uses energy from the water flowing downstream and converts it to kinetic energy within a turbine to generate electricity (Hydroelectricity, 2021). Hydroelectric systems can operate 24 hours a day and provide enough electricity to use the appliances in your home and power lighting, heating, and water heater. This electricity will be provided at a lower cost and without releasing harmful toxins into the air or the ground.

A hydroelectric system installed in your home can cost around $20,000 (Green Living Nation, n.d.). The cost of a hydroelectric system will depend on your home's equipment, labor, and location; maintenance costs are also low, with a system lasting 40–50 years after installation. This is an ideal and cost-effective kind of renewable energy for off-grid homes. So, look around where you live and see if there is a body of water you can take advantage of.

Wind Energy

Not many people know that you can harness wind power as a renewable energy source for your home. This is because this type of energy is often associated with larger commercial farms. If you live in a windy area, you can take advantage of wind power. If your home is far from urban areas, you can use this renewable energy option, especially if your home is off-grid.

A large wind turbine system for your home may be quite costly to install. If you consider using a small kit for supplementing your energy bank, it will cost significantly less ($1,000 - $4,000). Living in an area that often experiences wind traveling at 14 mph or more could mean you quickly see a return on investment. If you install a wind power system while living in a windy city, you can slash your power bill by as much as 90% (Price to Compare, n.d.). Several considerations exist for installing a wind energy system, including wind obstructions like trees or other buildings, whether the average wind includes gusts or steady wind, and lightning. Make sure to do your research before you invest in a wind turbine for energy.

Small wind turbine kits can help supplement your renewable energy supply.
Photo by Anders Sandberg

Codes and Requirements for Renewable Energy Systems in the Home

Depending on where you live, your local authority may have a set of codes, regulations, or requirements that you may need to adhere to before you install your renewable energy system (Planning for home renewable energy systems, n.d.). You may not even be allowed to install the type of renewable energy system you are leaning toward. Therefore, make sure you do your research before you get started. Your renewable energy system may be connected to your home outside of the electricity grid, or it may need to be plugged into it, and this may need permission from your local electric utility company. When I installed solar for my home, I was forced to plug into the Los Angeles Department of Water and Power, so my extra energy is credited for times when I exceed my production. Some of my neighbors, however, are with Southern California Edison and receive a check for selling their power production.

To find out what requirements must be met to install your renewable energy system, you can consult local officials or a local renewable energy organization or expert. You may have to understand and navigate easements, building codes, local governments and ordinances, and technology-specific requirements. Building and electrical inspectors may have to check your renewable energy system to ensure it is up to standard. The structure you are putting into place to support your renewable energy system needs to be safe, and there may be certain electrical or plumbing inspections that need to be carried out to make sure that the system and its structure are in line with local building codes.

You may need to apply for an easement if your renewable energy system needs to run through your neighbor's land. An easement is a legally-binding agreement granted to you voluntarily by your adjacent landowners, stating that you can use the adjoining land. Even if the adjacent land changes ownership, the agreement remains in place.

It is important always to search your title deed and look for easements or agreements that could prevent you from installing a renewable energy system on your property. Certain places can dictate, via regulation, what a homeowner can do on their property, and this power can extend to whether or not you can install and use renewable energy systems. The reasons for these kinds of regulations are usually to minimize noise or control the community's aesthetic. If a homeowner's association governs your community, check their regulations before investing in a renewable energy system. Discuss your plans with your neighbors to avoid future conflict. If you consult a local expert, they can break down the requirements for the specific renewable energy system you want to use in your home or point you in the right direction to the relevant local authority.

The Future Is Powered by Solar Power

Solar power is gaining popularity for a reason. It is versatile, accessible, and affordable. It is easy to customize it for your home and energy needs. If you live in the right area, solar energy can be whatever you want it to be; your imagination will dictate the various ways you can take advantage of this type of renewable energy. You can use solar energy in your home to advance your sustainability goals in different ways.

Solar Panels

Solar panels are the most common way people worldwide use solar power. You have probably noticed more and more roofs that have solar panels. "Photovoltaic cells within solar panels absorb sunlight and generate an electrical current that can be sent for use, stored for later, or sold back to the electrical grid" (Campbell, 2020). Although solar panels are a popular choice, do your research and investigate if they will work for your living situation. Calculating your electricity needs is the first step (Planning for home renewable energy systems, n.d.)

Solar Generators

If solar panels feel like too much of a financial burden, solar generators could be a more feasible solution for your home. A solar generator can provide renewable energy (not the same amount as a solar panel system) for your home to power small appliances. They are often portable and can be used as electric power banks to reduce the energy burden on your power supply.

Solar Attic Fans

Keeping your home cool in warm weather takes a lot of energy. Solar attic fans can help your cooling system work more efficiently by sharing the burden. What a solar attic fan does is suck up the hot air that may be present in your attic. If you have experience with handy work, DIY, or carpentry, you can save money by installing them yourself. Because solar attic fans are powered by solar energy, they don't add to your energy bill; you can save further because they qualify for a tax credit, meaning you will see a return on investment faster.

Solar Heating

How your house is positioned can allow you to take advantage of solar heating. This is an ancient practice that has been used for centuries. The passive solar design uses the sun's rays to introduce warmth to a building. If you position your home correctly, it can ensure that it is adequately warmed during the winter and cooled during the summer, but this is also dependent on your geographical location and your ability to choose the orientation of your home. However, it is possible to consider adding or expanding energy-efficient windows or skylights in an already present home.

An active solar heating system utilizes sunlight to heat air or a liquid which is then used to heat the home. The building can be fitted with a central heating system, radiant floors, or radiators. Depending on your needs and budget, you can use a solar liquid heating system that transfers heat to your radiators to enjoy affordable heating during the winter.

Outdoor Solar Lights

Consider outdoor solar lights to power your garden lights or any lighting outside your home. These light fixtures are fitted with a small solar panel on top of the light that absorbs light during the day and uses that solar energy to light up at night. Solar lights usually have no power cables, do not need to be installed by a professional, and are also quite affordable. You only have to remember to place them where they will have full access to the sun.

Benefits of a Home with Solar Energy

Besides the obvious energy savings you'll gain, there are other advantages to using solar panels in your home. Due to most systems having durable batteries that can serve as a backup, you never have to worry about power outages when you have a solar panel system. Further, because panels become permanent fixtures in your home, they add value to your home. You can expect your property value to increase by $15,000 after installing solar panels (Rosas, 2021). If you ever want to sell your home, this renewable energy feature may make it more desirable to eco-conscious buyers. A solar-powered home will also ease the energy burden on the electric grid, reducing the amount of electricity needed for the area.

Get Ahead of the Cold

When winter comes around, it can be hard to conserve energy. You may have the kettle going several times a day to enjoy a hot beverage that will warm you up. You may also want to use the furnace in your home to keep the indoor temperature warm and toasty at all times, but there may be better choices to make to stay eco-friendly.

You can do things to keep your sustainability habits going throughout the winter months and avoid using excessive amounts of energy. The first thing you can do is to seal your air leaks. Warmth escapes through small cracks beneath the door or your windows, resulting in you needing more energy to keep your house warm. Check if there are any leaks around your front or back doors, then inspect your windows and baseboards. You can successfully seal air leaks around your home using window kits, foam rods, caulking guns, rubber weather strips, and draft blockers.

You can program your thermostat to be at a lower temperature when no one is home or when you are tucked into your warm bed. Any slight decrease in temperature on the thermostat can save you money on your energy bill (Moulin, 2019). Keep your heating system up-to-date by having it checked every year. If you experience freezing weather, an efficient heat pump, furnace, or boiler won't get overworked and use too much energy.

Also, you don't always have to turn up the heat when it gets chilly. Remember to dress in layers; wear a scarf, thermal vests or undergarments, and wool hats and gloves. If you have blinds or drapes over your windows, pull them back to allow natural light and warmth in. I have honeycomb blinds to provide better insulation for when it is cold. Avoid using salt or chemicals to de-ice, as they can contaminate groundwater. Use snow shovels and brooms to clear walkways of ice and snow instead of fuel-powered machines.

How you choose to use renewable energy to power your home is entirely up to you. You can start small and use it to only power certain aspects of your home, like the lighting or the heating, before eventually moving on to more extensive renewable energy systems that can support your entire home's energy needs. Do not rush into any decisions, and be creative about the choices you make for your home. In time, you will be like a wind turbine—a big fan of energy efficiency.

Conclusion

Maybe you have been struggling to find ways to be more sustainable in your life. Sometimes it can be hard to personalize general directions to be eco-friendly. Now that you have reached the end of this book, you have more specific solutions for being less wasteful in all areas of your life.

You can now reduce food waste because this book has given you methods of food preservation so that you can stretch out supply if you have high yields. You don't have to wonder where to get water because you can now harvest water for yourself. You also know how to use your available space for farming in your backyard or on your balcony. The 5Rs form the basis of zero-waste, and you can now apply them to your daily life.

People think sustainability is daunting because they believe it will cost money when the reality is that it will save you a lot more than you will spend. After absorbing all the knowledge in each chapter, you can now start to save money as you make your life less about consumerism and more about being environmentally conscious. Eating the right food using eco-friendly production methods can also improve your health. With these kinds of benefits, I am hoping you are excited to get started on transforming your life. I encourage you to share this information with your family, friends, and neighbors so that those who are like-minded can go forth and make their lives more sustainable. It will "take a village" for the world to adopt a more sustainable approach to using the earth's natural resources.

Embarking on this journey requires determination, courage, and foresight, and I want to thank you for committing to change. It didn't matter when the moment that inspired change within you happened; what matters is that it happened. You decided to make the environment a priority in your life. You never have to lie awake at night wondering if you are doing enough. You can now be self-reliant and do your best to reduce the waste your household produces. I am sure you will have fun coming up with your own creative solutions to add to the ones described in this book. For yourself, your children, and those who come after us, you have made the right choice, and I know you won't regret it.

My love for being eco-friendly and sustainable came while pursuing a Ph.D. in wildlife biology. I realized that our society needs to do more to conserve natural resources and our environment. I was concerned that we were destroying the world at a rate that could not be stopped. My viewpoint has become more positive because I have seen more focus on sustainability and understand that multiple small efforts are just as crucial as one big one. This means that the onus is also on each one of us.

My consumerism levels have been drastically reduced, I eat what I grow and love shopping at the local non-profit thrift store. I was lucky enough to be able to invest in solar and now have no electric bill. I always find ways to repurpose or recycle my waste so that I do not add to the already existing environmental problems. I still have a long way to go and have yet to be able to incorporate all of the ideas I describe in this book, but I am excited to keep moving forward. I hope you, too, will become excited about moving toward a more sustainable lifestyle.

This book has given you some simple hacks that can help make your life more sustainable while saving money and teaching you how to be self-reliant. I hope you feel relieved and guided on the road ahead because you know where to start. Remember, I did not write this book to make you feel guilty but to empower you. Do what you can, and I am sure you will find more that you can do.

Also, remember that this is a lifelong road, so you must keep the consistency going. If you do what is right, not only for yourself but also for others and the environment, you will make a difference and set an example for others.

Which sustainable methods are you excited to implement first? Do you have a picture of where your garden will be and which vegetables you will plant? Always remember that you will live a better life in a better environment.

Leave a Review

The state of the environment gives feedback on how we have been treating it. Similarly, I would like you to leave a review on Amazon about this book so I know how it affected you. I would love to know your favorite parts and which pieces of information excited you. Your opinion matters to me because I wrote the book to help people. I wanted you to have a clear and cohesive solution for many of your sustainability problems. Your review is also instrumental in guiding people toward purchasing this book and giving them insight on whether or not it is a valuable tool on the road to becoming a zero-waste individual. I do hope you are happy with your investment. You should always go green, even if your efforts remain unseen. Share the idea of sustainability and this book because the planet and future generations need you! Thank you.

References

afox. (2019, March 2). *5 significant benefits of using energy-efficient appliances. Astral Energy.* https://www.astralenergyllc.com/5-significant-benefits-of-using-energy-efficient-appliances/

Akart, B. (2023, January 21). *Do you have a preppers mentality?* Freedom Preppers. http://www.freedompreppers.com/preppers-mentality.htm

Amy. (2017, May 18). *12 steps to preventing garden pests naturally.* Tenth Acre Farm. https://www.tenthacrefarm.com/preventing-garden-pests/

Ashley. (2014, June 30). *How to reuse 13 things you would normally throw away.* My Heart Beets. https://myheartbeets.com/reuse-13-things-normally-throw-away/ Aubury,

Aubrey, A. (2023, February 5*). Eggs prices drop, but the threat from avian flu isn't over yet:* NPR https://www.npr.org/sections/health-shots/2023/02/05/1153434486/eggs-prices-drop-but-the-threat-from-avian-flu-isnt-over-yet.

Baker, L. (2019, May 7). *10 home items you can reuse over and over again.* One Green Planet. https://www.onegreenplanet.org/lifestyle/home-items-you-can-reuse-over-and-over-again/

Barcal, L. (2022). *How to make your own beauty products.* WikiHow. https://www.wikihow.com/Make-Your-Own-Beauty-Products

Barton, R. (2013, June 6). *Know your garden soil: How to make the most of your soil type.* Eartheasy. https://learn.eartheasy.com/articles/know-your-garden-soil-how-to-make-the-most-of-your-soil-type/

Batista, C. (2020, November 28). *What is compostable at home? Over 100 ways to reduce waste!* The Eco Hub. https://theecohub.com/what-is-compostable/

Batista, C. (2022, September 5). *Do you know how to avoid microplastics in food?* The Eco Hub. https://theecohub.com/how-to-avoid-microplastics-in-food/

Beauchamp, E. (2018, January 25). *The beginner's guide to urban beekeeping.* Today's Homeowner. https://todayshomeowner.com/lawn-garden/guides/guide-to-urban-beekeeping/

Brooke. (2020, November 9). *10 benefits of eating organic food.* The Organic Place. https://www.theorganicplace.com.au/10-benefits-eating-organic-food/

Bueno, F. G. (2022, April 13). *5 DIY projects to kickstart your sustainable lifestyle.* Pinoy Builders. https://pinoybuilders.ph/diy-projects/

Brundtland, G.H. (1987, March 20). *Report of the World Commission on Environment and Development: Our Common Future.* Oslo. chrome-extension://efaidnbmn-nnibpcajpcglclefindmkaj/https://sustainabledevelopment.un.org/content/documents/5987our-common-future.pdf

Buzby, Jean. (2022, January). *Food Waste and its Links to Greenhouse Gases and Climate Change.* https://www.usda.gov/media/blog/2022/01/24/food-waste-and-its-links-greenhouse-gases-and-climate-change #:~:text=EPA%20estimated%20that%20each%20year,42%20coal-fired%20power%20plants.

Byrne, C. (2022, April 13). *What does a sustainable diet look like? Here's what the science says.* Healthline. https://www.healthline.com/nutrition/sustainable-eco-friendly-diet#focus-on-plant-foods

Can Alzheimer's disease be prevented. (2023, n.d.). Alzheimer's Association. https://www.alz.org/alzheimers-dementia/research_progress/prevention?utm_source=google&utm_medium=paidsearch&utm_campaign=google_grants&utm_content=alzheimers&gad=1&gclid=CjwKCAjw67ajBhAVEiwA2g_jELex-1PqliVWEsol6UdKfCzScaOtN5uLw1z8mFvybPtt5VYq7yt1pExoCh1QQAvD_BwE

Campbell, A. (2019, November 28). *29 natural ways to get rid of bugs on plants.* Dre Campbell Farm. https://drecampbell.com/how-get-rid-bugs-plants-naturally/

Campbell, U. (2020, May 29). *5 ways to use solar energy as a renewable energy source.* Biofriendly Planet. https://biofriendlyplanet.com/green-alternatives/solar/5-ways-to-use-solar-energy-as-a-renewable-energy-source/

Cap, S., Bots, P., & Scherer, L. (2022). *Environmental, nutritional and social assessment of nuts.* Sustainability Science. https://doi.org/10.1007/s11625-022-01146-7

Cheesman, D. (2020, October 5). *What is sustainable living?* The Good Trade. https://www.thegoodtrade.com/features/sustainable-living-definition

Chelsea. (2020, April 29). *Low impact living: A beginner's guide to sustainability.* Low Impact Love. https://lowimpactlove.com/low-impact-living/

Collins, P. (2021, October 28). *Sustainable transport: What is it and why is it important?* Selectra. https://climate.selectra.com/en/advice/sustainable-transport

Daman, B. (2019). *14 ways to reduce water waste.* Green Action Centre. https://greenactioncentre.ca/reduce-your-waste/14-ways-to-reduce-water-waste/

Dickson, C. (2022, June 29). *How to plant a garden for pollinators – in 10 insect-friendly steps.* Homes and Gardens. https://www.homesandgardens.com/gardens/garden-for-pollinators

Ebadi, S. W. Willett, and G.A. Stordalen. (2015, March 26). Huffington Post. *An American Plate That Is Palatable for Human and Planetary Health.* https://www.hsph.harvard.edu/nutritionsource/2015/06/17/5-tips-for-sustainable-eating/

Ellsmoor, J. (2019, July 23). *77% of people want to learn how to live more sustainably.* Forbes. https://www.forbes.com/sites/jamesellsmoor/2019/07/23/77-of-people-want-to-learn-how-to-live-more-sustainably/?sh=58cf64082b01

Elstad, S. (2022, February 14). *Can hydrogen cars still power the future of sustainable transportation?* Greener Ideal. https://greenerideal.com/news/vehicles/hydrogen-cars-sustainable-transportation/

Ettinger, J. (2021, December 6). *The healthiest diet is also the most sustainable one, health and climate experts agree.* Green Queen. https://www.greenqueen.com.hk/healthiest-diet-most-sustainable/

Ewald, J. (2014, August 7) *What is canning and what are the benefits?* Life and Health Network. https://lifeandhealth.org/lifestyle/what-is-canning-and-what-are-the-benefits/172324.html?gclid=Cj0KCQjwr82iBhCuARIsAO0EAZzlCRUdA-YyjkLdv9mDb6WXnCjoI5yAhz19JnyP8CFYZlZqAJdL1uMaAqVPEALw_wcB

"5 simple ways to stop wasting water around the house." (2018, March 3). Blog.kitchenandbathclassics.com. https://blog.kitchenandbathclassics.com/stop-wasting-water

"14 easy ways to start living a zero waste lifestyle." (2022, July 12). The Honest Consumer. https://www.thehonestconsumer.com/blog/how-to-live-a-zero-waste-life

FutureLearn (2022, October 25). *The three pillars of sustainability*. The University of Nottingham online course, Sustainability, Society, and You. https://www.future-learn.com/info/courses/sustainability-society-and-you/0/steps/4618

Garrity, A. and A. Gautieri (2023, April 21). 20 *Best Air-Purifying Plants to Infuse Greenery Into the Home*. https://www.goodhousekeeping.com/home/gardening/a32552/houseplants-that-purify-air/

Godman, H. (2022, December 1). *Walking linked to lower dementia*. Harvard Health Letter. https://www.health.harvard.edu/mind-and-mood/walking-linked-to-lower-dementia-risk.

Green Journal (2018, February 4) *How you can save money via green living DIY projects*. GreenJournal.co.uk. https://www.greenjournal.co.uk/2018/02/how-you-can-save-money-via-green-living-diy-projects/

Green Living Nation. (n.d.). The cost of a micro hydropower system (it's less than you think!). Green Living Nation. https://greenlivingnation.com/micro-hydropower-system-cost/

Greenbaum, H. and D. Rubinstein (2012, April 27). *Who Made That Mason Jar?* New York Times. https://www.nytimes.com/2012/04/29/magazine/who-made-that-mason-jar.html

Hirsh, S. (2022, March 1). *11 of our favorite eco-conscious celebrities and famous families*. Green Matters. https://www.greenmatters.com/p/eco-celebrities

Hisham, A. (2021, November 15). *What to buy and what to avoid at thrift shops*. G.O. Banking Rates. https://www.gobankingrates.com/saving-money/shopping/buy-and-avoid-thrift-store/

Houston, B. (2022, August 17). *Organic vs. non-organic food: What's the difference?* The Check Up. https://www.nib.com.au/the-checkup/organic-vs-non-organic-food-whats-the-difference#:~:text=Non%2Dorganic%20food%20%E2%80%93%20also%20known

Hubbard, A. (2022, September 23). *18 easy and green DIY recipes to clean all the things, plus health benefits*. Healthline. https://www.healthline.com/health/easy-green-diy-recipes-to-clean-all-the-things-plus-health-benefits#recipes

Huffstetler, E. (2019, November 20). *You can save more money at thrift stores with these easy tips*. LiveAbout. https://www.liveabout.com/save-more-money-at-thrift-stores-1389263

Hydroelectricity. (2021, September 7). Energy Saving Trust. https://energysavingtrust. org.uk/advice/hydroelectricity/

Jabs, B. (2012, September 13). *10 ways to live more sustainably.* DIY Natural. https:// diynatural.com/what-is-sustainable-living/

Jacobson, D. I., and Madden, H. (2023, May 6). *How to be buried as a tree.* Wiki-How. https://www.wikihow.com/Be-Buried-As-a-Tree.

Johnson, B. (2013, April 1). *Zero Waste Home: The Ultimate Guide to Simplifying Your Life by Reducing Your Waste.* Scribner 304 pp. https://www.goodreads.com/ book/show/15802945-zero-waste-home

Johnson, C. (2021, *September* 9). *7 ways to preserve your garden harvest.* Earth911. https:// earth911.com/home-garden/forever-food-7-ways-to-preserve-your-garden-harvest/

Johnson, N. (2023, March 13) *Beautiful nasturtium flowers keep bad bugs away.* Birds&Blooms. https://www.birdsandblooms.com/gardening/flower-gardening/ nasturtiums-or-nose-twisters/

Kelsey. (2021, November 22). *Top 9 common ways you are wasting water.* Advantage Plumbing & Sewer Co. https://www.advantageplumbingnow.com/2021/11/22/ ways-of-wasting-water-at-home/

Lamkin, P. (2023, February 15) *Best smart home hubs 2023: Do more by picking the perfect hub.* The Ambient. https://www.the-ambient.com/buyers-guides/ best-smart-home-hubs-2599

Loewe, E. (2023a, March 24). *2022's dirty dozen & clean 15 lists are out: Here's what to know.* Mind Body Green. https://www.mindbodygreen.com/articles/ ewg-dirty-dozen-and-clean-15-lists

Loewe, E. (2023b, April 21). *Unpacking what it means to eat sustainably: Food lists & pro tips to get you started.* Mind Body Green. https://www.mindbodygreen.com/ articles/sustainable-eating-plan

Londen Insurance Group, Inc. (2023) *How much does a funeral cost?* Lincoln Heritage Life Insurance Company. https://www.lhlic.com/consumer-resources/ average-funeral-cost/#:~:text=The%20average%20funeral%20costs%20 between

Lovely, L. (2022, June 22). *11 important things to know about clover lawns.* Bob Vila. https://www.bobvila.com/articles/clover-lawn/

Ly, L. (2021, October 5). *10 easiest vegetables to grow indoors year-round—no grow lights needed!* Garden Betty. https://www.gardenbetty.com/indoor-vegetables/

Mackenzie J. (2016, June 16). *Composting is way easier than you think.* Natural Resources Defense Council. https://www.nrdc.org/stories/composting-way-eas-ier-you-think?gclid=CjwKCAjw67ajBhAVEiwA2g_jEHOObkYj5uAFCppk-W9hGcHyXb5scEo6lh88fjoxx_7VsPT1xoswv-BoC5P4QAvD_BwE.

Mama Minimalist. (2018, March 6). *Your complete guide to homemade beauty products.* Sustainable Minimalists. https://mamaminimalist.com/homemade-beauty-products/

Marsh, J. (2020, May 13). *8 benefits of sustainable transportation.* Environment. https://environment.co/benefits-sustainable-transportation/

Martin, K. (2020, April 3). *12 easy vegetables to grow indoors.* Urban Garden Gal. https://www.urbangardengal.com/easy-vegetables-grow-indoors/

MasterClass. (2021, June 7). *Beginner's guide to recycling: 4 useful recycling tips.* MasterClass. https://www.masterclass.com/articles/how-to-recycle

Matthews, K. (2015, January 9). *8 ways to reduce your water waste.* Green Living Journal. https://www.greenlivingpdx.com/8-ways-to-reduce-water-waste/

Mayo Clinic Staff. (2020, August 20). *Vegetarian diet: How to get the best nutrition.* Mayo Clinic. https://www.mayoclinic.org/healthy-lifestyle/nutrition-and-healthy-eating/in-depth/vegetarian-diet/art-20046446

McKay, S. (2020, January). *Canning Foods at Home.* Clemson Cooperative Extension, Home and Garden Information Center. https://hgic.clemson.edu/factsheet/canning-foods-at-home/

Merriam-Webster (2023) *Prepper.* https://www.merriam-webster.com/dictionary/prepper

Miller, L. (2023, April 3). *How to get rid of the 10 worst garden insects.* Family Handyman. https://www.familyhandyman.com/list/10-worst-garden-insect-pests-and-how-to-get-rid-of-them/

Moulin, E. (2019, December 11). *How to live sustainably in the colder months.* Next Avenue. https://www.nextavenue.org/live-sustainably-colder-months/

Moxie. (2020, September 21). *16 interesting solar energy facts you probably didn't know.* Moxie. https://moxiesolar.com/2020/09/21/https-moxiesolar-com-blog-16-in-teresting-solar-energy-facts-you-probably-didnt-know/

Neverman, L. (2020, March 15). *Keep Deer Out of Your Garden – 5 Deer Deterrent Tips*. Common Sense Home. https://commonsensehome.com/keep-deer-out/

Neverman, L. (2021, March 16). *How to start a garden – 10 steps to gardening for beginners*. Common Sense Home. https://commonsensehome.com/start-a-garden/#4_8211_Invest_in_Basic_Garden_Tools

9 thrift shopping tips for saving money and the planet. (2023, May 4). Sustainable Jungle. https://www.sustainablejungle.com/sustainable-fashion/thrift-shopping-tips/

Painter, J., & Andı, S. (2020, June 16). *How much do people around the world care about climate change?* We surveyed 80,000 people in 40 countries to find out. The Conversation. https://theconversation.com/how-much-do-people-around-the-world-care-about-climate-change-we-surveyed-80-000-people-in-40-countries-to-find-out-140801

Peach, C. (2023, March 8). *10 tips to reuse items*. K.S. Environmental. https://ksenvironmental.com.au/10-tips-on-how-to-reuse-items/

Pesaturo, J. (2014, November 25). *How to start a backyard farm*. One Acre Farm. https://ouroneacrefarm.com/2014/11/25/start-backyard-farm/

Peterson, M. (2016, March 18). *Five steps of rainwater harvesting*. Monterey Coast Realty. https://www.montereycoastrealty.com/blog/five-steps-of-rainwater-harvesting-23.htm

Planning for home renewable energy systems. (n.d.). Energy Saver. https://www.energy.gov/energysaver/planning-home-renewable-energy-systems

Planting for pollinators. (2017, June 1). Kids Gardening. https://kidsgardening.org/resources/planting-for-pollinators/

Price to Compare. (n.d.). *The top 5 renewable energy sources for homes*. Price to Compare. https://www.pricetocompare.com/blog/renewable-energy-sources-for-homes/

Raja C. (2018, June 5). *Methods of rainwater harvesting | how to save rain water*. Mettur Diary. http://www.metturdiary.com/2018/06/methods-of-rainwater-harvesting-by-tamilnadu-government-method.html

Rinalducci, S. (2022, June 16). *The three pillars of sustainability explained*. Sustainability Success. https://sustainability-success.com/three-pillars-of-sustainability/

Rinalducci, S. (2023, May 2). *6 Rs of sustainability: Easy steps for a sustainable lifestyle*. Sustainability Success. https://sustainability-success.com/6-rs-of-sustainability-lifestyle-9-3-rs/

Rinkesh. (2014, January 24). *11 easy ways to make your home more energy efficient.* Conserve Energy Future. https://www.conserve-energy-future.com/11-ways-to-make-your-home-more-energy-efficient.php

Rinkesh. (2017, January 16). *Modes and benefits of green transportation.* Conserve Energy Future. https://www.conserve-energy-future.com/modes-and-benefits-of-green-transportation.php

Rinkesh. (2018, November 27). *Top ways to minimize water waste at home.* Conserve Energy Future. https://www.conserve-energy-future.com/ways-minimize-water-waste.php

Rosas, C. (2021, July 19). *What are the benefits of a solar-powered home?* Globe-Net. https://globe-net.com/what-are-the-benefits-of-a-solar-powered-home/

Savanah. (2016, June 9). *Natural pest control spray for your garden.* Midwest Modern Momma. https://midwestmodernmomma.com/natural-pest-control-spray-for-your-garden/?utm_campaign=coschedule&utm_source=pinterest&utm_medium=Midwest%20Modern%20Momma&utm_content=Natural%20Pest%20Control%20Spray%20For%20Your%20Garden

7 tips to recycle better. (2022, February 25). Earthday.org. https://www.earthday.org/7-tips-to-recycle-better/

17 simple home DIY projects that will save you money. (2019, April 19). Mid Penn Bank. https://midpennbank.com/home-diy-projects-that-save-money/

Siegel, S. (2020, July 13). *10 natural ways to eliminate garden insect pests.* Birds and Blooms. https://www.birdsandblooms.com/gardening/gardening-basics/natural-ways-eliminate-garden-insect-pests/

6 financial & environmental reasons why rainwater harvesting should be encouraged. (2017, December 6). Rainharvesting Systems. https://rainharvesting.co.uk/6-financial-environmental-reasons-rainwater-harvesting-encouraged/

State laws concerning backyard chickens. (n.d.). Omlet. https://www.omlet.us/guide/chickens/laws_about_keeping_chickens/state_laws/

Stella. (n.d.). *Sustainability facts: [20] fun facts about sustainable living.* Eco Friendly Habits. https://www.ecofriendlyhabits.com/sustainability-facts/

Swargari, N. (2021, October 13). *What future sustainable transportation holds for us?* Medium. https://medium.com/@namrata.interiors/what-future-sustainable-transportation-holds-for-us-228c2b210ea5

10 reasons why organic food is better for you and your clients. (2019, April 15). NESTA Certified. https://www.nestacertified.com/10-reasons-why-organic-food-is-better-for-you-and-your-clients/

The growth and feasibility of urban beekeeping. (2023, May 8). Perfect Bee. https://www.perfectbee.com/learn-about-bees/about-beekeeping/growth-of-urban-beekeeping

The Nature Conservancy. (2018, September 13). *Eight ways to reduce waste.* The Nature Conservancy. https://www.nature.org/en-us/about-us/where-we-work/united-states/delaware/stories-in-delaware/delaware-eight-ways-to-reduce-waste/

Thomas, Erin (October 2022) *Breakdown: Why scientists now say rainwater everywhere on Earth unsafe to drink.* https://www.actionnews5.com/2022/10/31/breakdown-why-scientists-now-say-rainwater-everywhere-earth-unsafe-drink/

Tips & tricks. (2023, May 8). Planet Natural. https://www.planetnatural.com/composting-101/tips/

Top 10 ways you're wasting water. (2014, October 15). Len the Plumber. https://lentheplumber.com/blog/top-10-ways-youre-wasting-water/

Trees.com Staff. (2018, September 16). *What is lawn aeration? When and how to do it?* Trees.com. https://www.trees.com/gardening-and-landscaping/lawn-aeration

25 nifty items you absolutely need to buy at thrift stores now. (2021, April 21). Duct Tape and Denim. https://ducttapeanddenim.com/25-things-always-buy-thrift-store/

Urban Abroad. (2022, September 25) *How to start an urban garden.* Urban Abroad. https://www.urbanabroad.com/how-to-start-urban-garden/

Vanderlinden, C. (2022, July 12) *The basics of Bokashi composting.* https://www.thespruce.com/basics-of-bokashi-composting-2539742

Voelcker, J. (2022, September 26). *Hydrogen fuel-cell vehicles: Everything you need to know.* Car and Driver. https://www.caranddriver.com/features/a41103863/hydrogen-cars-fcev/

Wales, M. (2019, January 28). *Why organic food is more sustainable.* Nature's Path Organic Foods. https://www.naturespath.com/en-us/blog/organic-food-sustainable/

Water conservation facts. (2019). Think H2O. https://www.thinkh2onow.com/water_conservation_facts.php

Weinert, J. (2022, March 1). *Mitigating the energy crisis with smart lighting.* Signify. https://www.signify.com/global/our-company/blog/sustainability/how-connected-lighting-can-help-resolve-the-energy-crisis#:~:text=IoT%2Denabled%20smart%20lighting%20can

Why sustainable living is so important? (2021, October 31). The Roundup. https://theroundup.org/why-sustainable-living-important/

Wight, K. (n.d.). *How eco-friendly tree pod burials work: Cost, process & impact.* Cake. https://www.joincake.com/blog/how-tree-pod-burials-work/

Will from Holland. (n.d.). *Sustainability doesn't have to be expensive.* Fool Proof Me. https://www.foolproofme.org/articles/724-sustainability-doesn-t-have-to-be-expensive

Worst, R. (2020, October 9). *Backyard farming for everyone: Get started easily today!* Worst Room. https://worstroom.com/backyard-farming/

Photos

Anders Sandberg from Oxford, UK - Vertical axis wind turbine, CC BY 2.0, https://commons.wikimedia.org/w/index.php?curid=7281895

Made in the USA
Columbia, SC
20 November 2024

47195034R00086